400 YEARS
OF POLISH IMMIGRANTS
IN AMERICA
1608 - 2008

EDITED BY

MARIUSZ M. BRYMORA

Washington 2008

Concept and edition Mariusz M. Brymora

The essay *Polish Contributions to American Life* and the biographies of T. Kosciuszko, K. Pulaski, Ch. Zabriskie, Fr. J. Dabrowski, H. Modjeska, R. Modjeski, J. Karge, W. Krzyzanowski, J.H. de Rosen, M. Bekker, C. Funk, F. Gabreski, J. Gronouski, J. Kosinski, B. Malinowski, S. Ulam, M. E. Zakrzewska and K. Ziolkowski written by James Pula

The essay *The Shortest History of Poles in America*, the biographies of J. Hofmann, J. Karski, J. Kiepura, R. Kuklinski, Liberace, Cz. Milosz, E. Muskie, P. Negri, J. Nowak, I. J. Paderewski, F. Piasecki, E. Piszek, A. Rubinstein and M. Sembrich-Kochanska, as well as the biographical entries in *More Icons* chapter written by Mariusz M. Brymora

Biographies of characters in *Icons of Today* chapter edited by Mariusz M. Brymora on the basis of the information provided by the characters themselves.

Cover design by Rafal Olbinski

Portraits of characters in *Icons of the Past* chapter by Marcin Bondarowicz

Photographs in *Icons of Today* chapter were provided by the characters described

The CD *Global Jamestown and the Poles* is part of Five CD Audio Series titled *New Perspective on Jamestown* produced by the Virginia Foundation for the Humanities and was provided by the American Institute of Polish Culture in Miami, FL

Financed by the Ministry of Foreign Affairs of the Republic of Poland

Washington 2008

Publisher *Ex Libris* Warsaw
Typesetting and formatting by Kuba Buragiewicz

ISBN : 1-928900-81-X
ISBN : 978-83-89913-47-0

Dear Friends,

Last year America celebrated the 400th anniversary of the settling of Jamestown, Virginia, the event that established a new culture which soon created the foundation of the American state. Many nations have contributed to building the United States of America. They are all proud that they could participate in creating the strongest democracy in the world - home of immigrants from every corner of the globe. So are we, Poles, to have been present in America since its earliest days. On October 1st, 1608 The Mary and Margaret brought the second load of Europeans to the New World, among them four Poles, artisans known for their ability to produce potash, soap ash, tar and other commodities.

Since those early days, generation after generation, Poles and Polish Americans worked with all their strength and ability "to form a more perfect Union, establish Justice, insure domestic Tranquility, provide for the common defense, promote the general Welfare, and secure the Blessings of Liberty" to themselves and their posterity.

It is my great pleasure, as the Minister of Foreign Affairs of Poland, an ally of the United States, to send my congratulations to the millions of Polish people who made their homes in America but retained their ties with Poland. I would like to express my appreciation to all those who welcomed my countrymen in the hospitable land of Abraham Lincoln with open arms and hearts.

Looking with pride at 400 years of the history of Polish immigrants in America, I invite you to read this album and meet my compatriots who have made an outstanding contribution to the United States of America.

With best regards,

With best regards,

Radoslaw Sikorski

Warsaw, June 2008

INTRODUCTION AND ACKNOWLEDGEMENTS

At a recent diplomatic function in Virginia I said to an American lawyer that the most striking difference between American and Polish societies is that the former is the most diverse in the world whereas the latter most homogeneous. "That is where we take our strength from", he replied promptly. It may as well be true. And even though one could argue that there are some other sources of the American strength, there is little - if any - doubt that this unique mixture of immigrants who settled here over the course of the last four centuries added a lot to the American democracy, political system, economic strength and even the way of life.

No one can deny the fact that Poles are among those who have played a significant role in the building of the American statehood, starting from the time of the first settlement at Jamestown, VA. Among the pilgrims who disembarked from *The Mary and Margaret* on October 1st, 1608 there were four Polish artisans who gave beginning to the 400-year-long period of activity of our compatriots in the process of creating America as we know it today. This book introduces one hundred individuals of Polish blood who stood out from millions of Poles in America due to their outstanding achievements which brought them fame and appreciation going far beyond their Polish communities. It is but a selection of Poles and Polish Americans whose exceptional past services rendered to the American society are remembered today as well as those whose contemporary accomplishments are bound to go down in the history of American science, culture, sports etc.

The selection of people presented in the album is by no means complete. Nor was it intended to be. To get a fuller account of what Poles have done for America we need to wait for the publication of the *Polish American History and Culture: An Encyclopedia* which is currently being prepared by members of the Polish American Historical Association (PAHA). This Encyclopedia will contain informative and interpretative essays as well as about one thousand biographical entries. *400 Years of Polish Immigrants in America* was conceived merely as an introductory attempt to highlight the contribution of Poles to the development of the U.S.

Hence, this book does not mention an impressive array of leaders of the Polish diaspora in the United States whose commitment and dedication have been instrumental for its members throughout its long history. Nor does it introduce hundreds of Polish veterans, academics, business people and many others who - for various reasons - made their way from Poland to America, lived successful lives and died here. Among contemporary characters in the album there are people from many walks of life - artists, scientists, athletes, etc. It is easily noticeable that there are no active politicians among them, even though people of Polish decent have clearly marked their presence on the political arena of this country: a long-standing Senior Senator from Maryland - Barbara Mikulski, the first ever woman Senator from Alaska - Lisa Murkowski, the 2nd longest serving Representative ever - John Dingell, the charismatic Senator from Nebraska, Chuck Hagel - to name but a few. I have left them out intentionally realizing that "tying" them to only one ethnic group would stand in contradiction to their fundamental duty to represent all residents of their congressional districts. The encyclopedic publication of PAHA will undoubtedly secure a well-deserved place for all these people.

Notwithstanding the above assumptions, the selection process proved very difficult and sometimes controversial. No wonder - with over 9.3 million people of Polish decent in America reported by the latest census and tens of millions who have lived here since 1608, I had a huge oversupply and a great challenge to face. After hours of debates and consultations with many friends who are experts on America, I finally came up with the list which proves representative enough to reflect the substantial contribution that Poles made to America through the lives and work of these individuals.

I would like to acknowledge here a few select people whose engagement was fundamental for the realization of this project. As its originator and editor, I owe my greatest thanks to the co-authors of this work: Prof. James Pula, Rafał Olbinski, and Marcin Bondarowicz without whose contribution this book would not have been possible. I also thank the characters of Icons of Today chapter for responding so favorably to my requests and for our fruitful cooperation.

I am very grateful to my friends from the American Institute of Polish Culture in Miami: Lady Blanka Rosenstiel and Beata Paszyc who made it possible to enrich the book with the CD on Poles in Jamestown.

A word of thanks must go to the publisher - EXLIBRIS Company in Warsaw - whose cooperation was crucially important in the realization of the project especially bearing in mind that we are on two different sides of the Atlantic Ocean.

In the course of editing this book I benefited from the wisdom of many people. I am very grateful to all those who patiently and politely listened to all my doubts, discussed them with me and offered their advice. I am especially grateful to Professor Andrzej Rabczenko for his priceless encouragement and assistance and Dr. Adam Janiszewski for his invaluable consultancy.

The publication of this book was made possible by the funds assigned for it by the Department of Promotion of the Polish Ministry of Foreign Affairs, so my thanks go to the colleagues in Warsaw.

Last but not least, I would like to express my sincere gratitude to my superiors: Minister of Foreign Affairs of the Republic of Poland Radoslaw Sikorski, Polish Ambassador in the U.S. Robert Kupiecki and Deputy Chief of Mission Wojciech Flera without the support of whom I could not have succeeded.

To all these people I extend my sincere thanks and appreciation in the hope that the Reader, our most important judge, will appraise the project as something of value.

Mariusz Brymora

Washington, June 2008

The Shortest History of Poles in America

by
Mariusz M. Brymora

Whatever source of information on the Polish diaspora one would use, there will be no doubt whatsoever about one point - the largest Polish community outside their own country has always been in the United States of America. People fled Poland to America to look for better living conditions, to avoid persecutions of the occupying forces or to find freedom when the Communist authorities decided to suppress *Solidarity* movement by the imposition of martial law. For Poles, America has always been a myth, a country which served as a model of democracy, tolerance, and equal rights, as well as the subject of their dreams about getting rich and hence the goal of their crusades in search for freedom and prosperity.

At the beginning of the year 2000, I was taking my first trip through the United States as a Polish Consul in Chicago. I was heading for Kearney, Nebraska, having been invited by the University of Nebraska to give a talk on political, social, and economic transformations in Poland after 1989. Before leaving Chicago I asked the organizers whether they thought it would be possible for me to meet some local Polish Americans, if there were any at all in that area. On the following morning I received a few similar e-mails. "Polish Americans?" they all said, "there are plenty of them around". The organizers were so efficient that they even found a Polish priest, father Stanley Gorak, who gladly agreed to be my guide especially that it was a very rare occasion for him to speak Polish a little. Being driven by a University driver and accompanied by my family and father Gorak, I set out for a meeting with the local Polish-American community. Some 40-50 miles north of the I-80 Interstate we reached a tiny town of Loop City. At its edge, to my great amazement, I spotted a huge wooden obelisk with an inscription: "Welcome to Loop City - Polish Capital of Nebraska; Polish Days 9-11 June". From Loop City we went on to an even smaller village of Ashton where a group of Polish Americans was patiently waiting for their first official guest from Poland in front of a small wooden house which they all were very proud of. A few months before they had bought the place and founded the Polish Heritage Center there to house a library and a small exhibition which displayed a number of Polish artifacts, including books, photographs, folk decorations and even … Polish tissues. Americans say about places like Loop City or Ashton that they are "in the middle of nowhere". And even though it seemed very true to me when I was there, I was warmly greeted by quite a big group of Polish Americans, proud of their ethnic roots and their Polishness. How did they get there, then? Nebraska was admitted to the Union shortly after the end of the Civil War, in 1867. At that time the American government, wanting to encourage people to move west, gave away land on the territory which today is the state of Nebraska and then was the Wild West. Some entrepreneurial Poles from the big cities of the eastern coast or from Chicago decided to go. Others followed suit and settled close by, simply to overcome the fear of being alone. This was how the first all-Polish settlements were founded in the Cornhusker State. Two and a half centuries later, meeting the fifth or even sixth generation descendents of those people during my memorable trip across the wilderness of Nebraska became irrefutable evidence for me that Poles can be found everywhere in America.

Mieczyslaw Heiman - one of the best known and most trustworthy historians of Poles in America - distinguishes three main periods of immigration from Poland:

1. Colonial immigration, 1608-1776
2. Political immigration, 1776-1865
3. Economic immigration, 1865-1975 (i.e. the time of the publication of his book *Polish Past in America*).

While his division is to a large extent symbolic, there do exist certain characteristics of particular periods of immigration. Simultaneously with the time division, Heiman introduced a kind of "quality" division of the Polish immigration dividing it into political (well educated people who came here in pursuit of higher goals) and economic (impoverished and uneducated Poles who came to America empty-handed).

There are legends saying that the first Polish explorers came to America even before Christopher Columbus time. Legend has it that a Pole took part in a Columbus expedition, but there is no historical evidence to prove it. The situation looks much better when it comes to the Jamestown colony in Virginia from the beginning of the 17th century. There were no Poles among the group which founded the first permanent English settlement in 1607. However, a year later, on October 1, 1608, the British ship *Mary and Margaret* brought to Virginia a group of 70 settlers and among them four Polish craftsmen who immediately set up facilities for producing glass, pitch, soap ashes and other commodities which they soon started exporting to England. In 1609 they made their name by saving the life of the colony's President John Smith who was captured by the Indians. Later ships brought to Virginia more Poles who stood out from all the settlers both defending the colony against hostile Indians and developing its craft. Ten years later the Poles of Jamestown started what in modern terms could be called civil rights movement. They went on strike demanding equal rights with the English. Upon the decision of the Company's authorities in London "it was now agreed (…) that they shall be enfranchised and made as free as any inhabitant there whatsoever: and because their skill in making pitch and tar and soap ashes shall not die with them, it is agreed that some young men shall be put into them to learn their skill and knowledge therein for the benefit of the country hereafter."[1]

Polish peasants, traders and workers were among those who came to New Holland, which later became the State of New York, during the second half of the 17th century. At about the same time first Poles came to New England. One of them was Olbracht Zaborowski who soon became a very wealthy man and was appointed the first Justice of the Peace in Upper Bergen County in New York State. One of his grandsons, Christian Brevoot Zabriskie became Vice President of Pacific Coast Borax Company. The famous Zabriskie Point in the Death Valley was named after him.

Soon afterwards the Poles moved westwards. Accounts from the first half of the 18th century confirm their presence in Pennsylvania, Ohio, and Kentucky. In 1776 and 1777 two most famous Poles - Tadeusz Kosciuszko and Kazimierz Pulaski - came to America. The purpose of their trip here was - in Pulaski's own words, spoken to President George Washington - "to serve freedom and to live or die for it". The fame of these two Poles in America is enormous. They have their monuments and busts; towns and villages as well as numerous streets, schools, parks and other places across the country bear their names. It seems that Pulaski leads the unofficial rivalry for popularity between the two simply because his name is easier for Americans to pronounce. Historical sources report that there were about a hundred Poles fighting in the American War of Independence. Pulaski was promoted to a brigadier general and

---

[1] *The records of the Virginia Company*, vol. I, p. 251 in Miecislaus Heiman, *Polish Past in America*, Chicago 1974, p. 15

made the ranking officer in charge of the newly formed cavalry contingent. His subsequent exceptional accomplishments brought him the title of "the Father of the American Cavalry". He was fatally wounded during the siege of Savannah, GA in 1779. Kosciuszko earned his fame not only for serving as the chief military engineer of the Revolutionary War but also for designing West Point fortifications. What is more, upon his departure from America in 1798, he left behind his famous will in which he authorized his friend Thomas Jefferson to use all his American assets to free and educate black slaves.

Meanwhile in 1790 the first census was organized in America. Its results, even though partial, justify the claim that there were about 500 Poles in this country at that time. At the turn of the century an outstanding Polish writer Julian Ursyn Niemcewicz spent almost eight years in the United States. He travelled a lot and then described his American experiences in his memoir titled *Under Their Vine and Fig Tree: Travels Through America in 1797-1799, 1805, with Some Further Account of Life in New Jersey*. Niemcewicz became acquainted with President Washington, paid a long visit to Mount Vernon in 1798, and after returning to Poland published a book which in fact was the first biography of George Washington.

The first half of the 19th c. saw a relatively small influx of Poles into America. They were mainly veterans of the Napoleonic Wars and of the Polish November Uprising of 1830. The circumstances of their departure from Poland as well as the social status they enjoyed there made them political defectors. In the spring of 1834 a large group of over 200 people from Poland was coming to America. While still on board of their vessel, they founded the Polish Committee in America which can be considered the first Polish organization in the United States. Also in 1834 the first Polish book (a textbook of English for Poles) was published in Philadelphia and was meant to be used by the pupils of the first Polish school in the country run by the author of the book, Martin Rosienkiewicz. The first Polish periodical, titled *Poland - Historical, Literary, Monumental and Picturesque*, appeared in New York in 1842, but it was not until 1863 when the first Polish newspaper *Echo z Polski* (*Echo from Poland*) was launched, also in New York.

From the mid 19th c. immigration from Poland gradually acquired an economic character. The first organized groups of Poles who arrived here to seek a better life came to Texas in 1854. Under the leadership of Leopold Moczygemba, a Franciscan priest, they founded the first Polish settlements in America and named them after our religious symbols - Panna Maria (Virgin Mary) and Czestochowa (the name of the religious capital of Poland). Soon afterwards the 8th census reported 7,300 Poles in the U.S., living mostly in New York, Texas and California (a third of their total number was west of the Mississippi river). It is generally agreed that the number of Poles disclosed in all the censuses of the 19th century was understated because immigrants coming to the United States were registered on the basis of their citizenship or the harbor where they embarked on ships to America. Thus many Poles were put down as citizens of the countries which partitioned Poland, or as Germans because this was where they most often started their journeys across the Atlantic. The real number of Poles in America at the beginning of the Civil War is estimated at thirty thousand. Most of them lived in the North and, naturally, when the war broke out, they took the side of the Union. About five thousand Poles fought in the war, sometimes against one another, but they remained loyal to their respective sides. Among over one hundred Polish officers were a few colonels and three generals, including Union brigadier generals Wlodzimierz Krzyzanowski and Joseph Karge. In the Confederate States Army the most famous officer of Polish descent was Kasper Tachman who reached the rank of a colonel.

The rising number of Poles, who brought with them the Roman Catholic heritage, was reflected by the foundation of the first Polish church in America - St. Stanislaw Kostka church in Chicago in 1866. It was shortly followed by the Holy Trinity Church (1873) which still remains one of the most important centers of both religious and social life of Poles in the Windy City.

A huge wave of economic immigration from Poland started in the 1870s. Until the outbreak of World War I over two million Poles came to America, a vast majority of them through the most famous gate to the "Promised Land" - Ellis Island. This was also the time when the first Polish organizations in America were founded, including the Polish Roman Catholic Union of America (1873) and the Polish National Alliance (1880), which have been continuously in operation until the present time.

The official census data for the year 1900 reported some 700,000 Poles in America, with Illinois, New York and Pennsylvania being the most Polish states. Only between 1899 and 1915, the time of the highest economic immigration from Poland, over 1.4 million Poles were admitted to the United States. Most of them were young people who came to America to seek a better life. Three partitions of Poland, a number of unsuccessful attempts to regain independence, persecutions by the invaders, and finally poverty and no prospects for a better life, were the main causes responsible for making the 19th c. the time of "great emigration" from Poland. The census of 1910 reported almost 1.7 million Poles, divided into those born in Poland (c. 938,000) and those born in America whose at least one parent was born in Poland (c. 726,000). These figures, however, were rather conservative and definitely below the actual number of Poles. The Polish National Alliance Calendar for that same year estimated the number of Poles to be over 3 million and listed Pennsylvania, New York, Illinois, Wisconsin, and Michigan as the states with the biggest populations of Polish Americans. The year 1910 saw the first demonstration of the political power of the Polish diaspora in the United States. From May 10 until May 14, the Polish National Congress was held in Washington D.C. Over 400 delegates, accompanied by a few thousand supporters, manifested their strength in the American capital while their homeland remained unmarked on the map of Europe. The underlying reason behind the congress was to unveil the monuments of Kazimierz Pulaski and Tadeusz Kosciuszko, Polish heroes of the American War of Independence.

During World War I immigration to the United States from Europe, including Poland was significantly reduced not only because of the turmoil that swept across Europe. In 1917, overruling the veto of President Wilson, the Congress passed the so called Literacy Law. Soon afterwards American ports of entry were equipped with the signs which read:"If you cannot read, do not enter". Almost a third of Poles who came here between 1898 and 1914 fell into the category of the illiterate. Nor were they financially fit. On average each of them had less than 14 dollars in their pockets.

The second decade of the 20th c. was the height of political activity of Ignacy Jan Paderewski - composer and pianist of international reputation and also a statesman and Prime Minister of Poland. His ceaseless efforts brought about the involvement of President Woodrow Wilson in the campaign for independence of our country. The President's famous speech in which he stated, "Take it for granted that statesmen everywhere are agreed that there should be a united, independent, autonomous Poland", turned into point 13 of Wilson's 14 point plan for the world, which helped our country regain independence after 123 years of partitions. At the same time Polish Americans started acquiring political power. In 1918 Mr. John Kleczka became the first member of the Congress of Polish descent. Interestingly enough, he represented the GOP while, throughout history, over 75% of Polish representatives in Congress were Democratic.

In 1919, following the establishment of diplomatic relations between Poland and the United States, the Polish legation was opened in Washington at 2640 16th Street, in the building which, after almost 90 years, still is the seat of the Embassy of Poland. Consulates General in New York and Chicago as well as in Buffalo, Detroit, and Pittsburgh were established with the task to look after the growing population of Poles in America. By 1920 it reached 4 million, with major centers in Chicago, Detroit, Milwaukee, Buffalo, Pittsburg, New York, and Philadelphia. In the 1920s, a considerable number of them returned to independent Poland. At the same time the American Congress passed the Restriction Acts of 1921 and 1924 which limited the flow of immigrants into the USA. Notwithstanding these facts, the number of Poles in America continued to grow until World War II.

The eight years between 1935 and 1943 saw the establishment of important Polish cultural institutions in the U.S. In 1935 the Polish Museum of America was opened in Chicago with Mieczyslaw Heiman as its first curator. In 1941 Oskar Halecki founded PIASA - Polish Institute of Arts and Sciences of America, and two years later the Pilsudski Institute started operating in New York. In 1944 over 2,500 delegates came to Buffalo for the first congress of the American *Polonia*.[2] They established the Polish American Congress as an organization whose aim was to unite *Polonia* and act on behalf of all Poles in America. PAC officially recognized the Polish Government-in-Exile, protested against the Soviet Union annexing the eastern part of Poland, and criticized the Yalta Conference decisions. Unfortunately, the newly born organization was not able to influence the position of President Roosevelt and the American administration in these matters.

A new wave of Polish immigrants reached America in the years following the end of World War II. Within but a few years about half a million of Poles came to the States as political exiles. The end of the war found them either in POW camps on the German territory or somewhere in Western Europe where they concluded their wartime wandering. They either did not want to go back to their homeland which found itself under the Soviet domination or they actually had nowhere to go back to as their home towns and villages were now part of the Soviet Union. This post-war wave of immigrants introduced the division into "old" and "new" *Polonia*. The latter strongly supported the Polish government in London and was openly hostile towards the Communist authorities in Warsaw, whereas some of the old *Polonia* (i.e. those who were born in America of Polish parents) were more likely to accept the new Polish authorities. Luckily such ideas never won among Polish Americans. Even though the new authorities in Warsaw tried hard to convince people to return, Poles in America remained uncompromising and strongly opposed the "new Polish deal". In 1948 the American Congress passed the Displaced Persons Act on the grounds of which over 150 thousand Poles entered the United States.

The 1950s, 1960s and 1970s was the time when immigration of Poles was effectively limited by the communist authorities to cases of family reunification. The birth of *Solidarity* - the first independent Trade Union Organization in Central and Eastern Europe - and its subsequent suppression following the introduction of martial law in 1981 brought about the latest wave of Polish immigration to America which is referred to as the *Solidarity* immigration. Those who came here in the 1980s were mostly intellectuals who had to flee Poland to avoid persecutions of the Communist regime.

The fall of the iron curtain in 1989 and the rebirth of democracy in Poland which followed did not stop the immigration of Poles to America. In the years 1991- 2003 over 200,000 people from Poland came to the United States. The latest census of the year 2000 reported 9.3 million people of Polish descent. The biggest Polish communities are located in the states of New York, Illinois, and Michigan. Chicago remains the favorite city for Poles who wish to settle down in America. In the last 20 years a considerable increase of the Polish population was reported in the South-Western states (mainly in Texas and Arizona) as well as in Florida. The present-day Polish community in the USA is well educated (one third of them hold a Bachelor's or higher degree), quite well off (the average annual income of a Polish family exceeds considerably the national average), and its members enjoy the status of home owners much more often than other Americans.

---

[2] Polish word used to describe all Poles living abroad

For many years LOT Polish Airlines representatives operating in the United States used to say that their planes brought more Poles to America than they took back. However, recent years indicate that we might be witnessing a historical change. Poland has gone through sweeping political, social and economic transformations which thoroughly changed the life of people there. We have joined the European Union, becoming one of the biggest member states. Poland's membership in the EU, in turn, opened for our people the gates to 26 other European countries where we can freely settle down and work. On top of that, the Polish currency got so strong against the American dollar that coming to America has lost much of its original appeal. Hence, all traditional reasons for emigrating from Poland to America, i.e. seeking political freedom, economic well being or escape from regime persecutions are gone. It may well mean that we are just going through a historical turning point which will mark a gradual fall in the number of Poles in America. Even if this proves true, however, the Polish people will always retain the distinctive place in the history of the United States of America which they secured in the last 400 years.

"Polish American Contributions to American Life"
by
James S. Pula

The United States has been described as a nation of nations, a country comprised of peoples who trace their varied origins to every geographic and political segment of the globe. American history and culture is, in fact, the sum total of contributions by all of the peoples who chose throughout its existence to make it the destination of their migration. Some came early, some arrived later. Polish Americans are fortunate that their heritage stretches back beyond even the nation's foundation, back to the first period of European settlement when Poles arrived in Jamestown, Virginia, only a year after the colony was founded, and when Poles arrived with the Dutch to settle New Amsterdam, a vibrant multi-national city even before it came into English possession as New York.

In Jamestown, four Poles arrived in 1608 as artisans skilled in the manufacture of potash, soap ash, tar, pitch, resin and other commodities in demand in England. In addition to manufacturing the first commercial products sent from the new English colony back to Europe, they also took part in the daily life of the colony. Early records of the colony show that two Poles saved the life of its president, John Smith, when he was attacked by an Indian "king", while another was killed in the Indian attack on the colony in 1622. Others, wishing to participate fully in the colony's political processes, lodged a complaint about a rule denying them the rights of citizenship. Exiting English records from the time indicate that the Poles stopped work until their grievances were addressed; thus, writers have often referred to this as the first "strike" in American history. The result was that the Poles were fully vested with the political rights enjoyed by English citizens, and in return they agreed to teach their skills to others for the greater benefit of the colony.

In New Amsterdam, Poles arrived with the Dutch as traders, soldiers, teachers, and ordinary settlers, the most famous of who was probably Olbracht Zaborowski who learned enough of the local Indian language to serve as an interpreter. Amassing a significant fortune, Zaborowski, or Zabriskie as it was later written, owned most of what is today Northern New Jersey and was named the first justice of the peace for that area. Anthony Sadowski headed another early Polish pioneer family. Along with his sons, this eighteenth century Pennsylvania settler explored westward into the Ohio Valley and what would later become Kentucky. Legend has it that the city of Sandusky, Ohio, bears a corrupted version of his original name.

With the outbreak of the American Revolution, Poles contributed significantly to the cause of liberty. Among the first European volunteers to arrive was Thaddeus Kosciuszko, an engineering officer, who quickly went to work designing fortifications along the river approaches to Philadelphia. Appointed a colonel of engineers, he played a crucial role in the American victory at the Battle of Saratoga, designed and constructed the first fortifications at West Point, and later made equally noteworthy contributions during the campaigns in the Carolinas under Gen. Nathanael Greene. After the war, he went back to Europe to lead his own unsuccessful uprising against Russian rule in Poland. Visiting the United States soon thereafter, he penned a will in which he left his American property to purchase the freedom of slaves and educate them for citizenship. He was truly, as described by Thomas Jefferson, a pure son of liberty.

Kazimierz Pulaski, already a veteran of an uprising in Poland against Russian occupation, arrived to lend his considerable military experience to the patriot cause first at the Battle of Brandywine where he helped prevent Gen. George Washington's army from being caught in a British trap, and then as "Commander of the Horse", a position that gave him the responsibility for training all American cavalry units, earning him the popular sobriquet "Father of the American Cavalry." His death leading a charge against the British at the Battle of Savannah, GA is commemorated each year on "Pulaski Day."

Poles served in the Legion of the Duc de Lucerne and other French forces that arrived to support the American colonists, but they also made contributions to American independence off the battlefield. Haym Salomon, a Jewish immigrant from Poland, served as the principle financial broker for the fledgling American government, often also loaning money to such patriot stalwarts as Alexander Hamilton and James Madison. Madison noted that Salomon "obstinately rejects all recompense" for his services. In Holland, the banking house of Pieter Stadnitski became the principle brokerage firm for American bonds, selling more securities to finance the American Revolution than any other business.

Following the Revolution, Poles continued to migrate to America, often exiles following further failed uprisings against the occupying powers. Among these political refugees were many people who made significant contributions to the development of the social causes that were becoming prominent in American life between 1830 and 1860. Ernestine Potocka Rose, for example, was largely responsible for the passage in New York of the first law in the United States allowing married women to own property in their own name rather than that of their husbands. Elizabeth Zakrzewska, one of the first female physicians in America, was a leader in establishing medical facilities for women and children, as well as supporting the growing anti-slavery movement. Adam Gurowski's seminal work *Slavery in History* was considered one of the best works on the subject when it was published in 1860. Thaddeus Lewinski was for years associated with anti-slavery newspapers, while Michael Heilprin, another anti-slavery advocate, later became an associate editor of the *American Cyclopœdia* and a regular contributor to the New York *Nation.* American culture was also enriched through the presence of several Polish artists and literary figures. The sculptor Henryk Dmochowski-Saunders created busts of Kosciuszko and Pulaski that were placed in the U.S. capitol building. Edward Sobolewski wrote *Mohega*, the first opera using for its theme the American Revolution. Casimir Gzowski engineered the first bridge spanning the Niagara Gorge, while Frederick Schwatka became an internationally known Arctic explorer.

With the outbreak of the Civil War, Polish Americans were forced to choose sides along with other Americans. Most chose to support the Union, seeing in it a reflection of the same freedoms that many of them had attempted to bring to their own homeland through unsuccessful uprisings in 1830, 1846 and 1848. Wlodzimierz Krzyzanowski rose to the rank of brigadier general while leading a brigade at Chancellorsville, Gettysburg and in the relief of Chattanooga and Knoxville. When the Union position at Gettysburg was threatened by a Confederate attack on Cemetery Hill on July 2, 1863, he led the first troops to respond to crisis and defeat the attack. Joseph Kargé also rose to brigadier general, leading cavalry units against the Confederacy and is said to have been the only Union cavalry officer to defeat Confederate Nathan Bedford Forest in an open fight. Albin Schoepf, also a brigadier general, led a division at the Battle of Perryville. Later, as commander of the prisoner of war camp at Fort Delaware, he won praise for his humanitarian administration. Hundreds of other Poles served the Union cause as engineers, signal officers, artillery commanders, and common soldiers. Edmund Zalinski, a lieutenant in the Union Army, was also a noted inventor who developed telescopic sights and range-finding instruments for artillery and the pneumatic dynamite torpedo. David Orbansky is believed to be the first

Polish American to be awarded the Medal of Honor for gallantry in action. Meanwhile, Poles who settled in the South often viewed the Southern struggle for independence as similar to the struggle of Poland for its independence. Col. Valerian Sulakowski led the 14th Louisiana Infantry, Lt. Col. Hipolite Oladowski served as chief of ordnance for Gen. Braxton Bragg's Confederate army, and many others served in various capacities in the South. The vast majority of Poles supported preservation of the Union and the elimination of slavery.

A dominant theme in postbellum American history was the expansion of industry with its associated effects on society, economics, politics and the emergence of organized labor. Poles formed the second largest single nationality group after Italians to migrate to America between 1880 and 1920, thus forming a very large percentage of the workforce that drove industrial expansion during this period. In keeping with the saying "For Our Freedom and Yours," the traditional motto of Poles fighting for freedom, from the beginning of the modern labor movement in the United States in the nineteenth century, Polish workers have played active roles in obtaining equal treatment and a better life for themselves and for all Americans. Indeed, many early union leaders were Poles. David Dubinsky became president of the International Ladies' Garment Workers' Union (ILGWU), was an active member of the group that eventually formed the Congress of Industrial Organizations (CIO) and a founder of the American Labor Party. Alexander Debski, who published the New York newspaper *Telegram Codzienny*, was a prominent labor activist, as was Leo Krzycki who served as a vice president of the CIO and president of the Socialist Party in America. Mary Zuk led a series of strikes in Michigan, becoming the first female president of a United Auto Workers local, while Joseph "Jock" Yablonski, a leader in the United Mine Workers, was murdered while he was running a reform campaign for union president. These are but a few of the more prominent Polish Americans who have led and supported the goals of organized labor in America. Between 1936 and 1938, it has been estimated that 500,000 to 600,000 Polish Americans joined the new CIO unions. They became, in the words of Homer Martin, the first president of the United Auto Workers, "the most militant and progressive workers" in America.

Another primary theme of the Gilded Age and Progressive Eras is the topic of immigration, with the struggles of people to adapt to lives in often startling new environments. Florian Znaniecki, from the original group of scholars who formed the well-known "Chicago School" of sociology, was one of the first researchers to examine the development of immigrant communities in the United States. Together with his colleague William I. Thomas, Znaniecki co-authored *The Polish Peasant in Europe and America*, a pioneering sociological study still in use in American university classrooms today. Another person who played a significant role during the same era was Rev. Waclaw Kruszka who promoted the idea of a pluralistic Catholic Church in America long before the concept of cultural diversity became widely accepted.

With the outbreak of World War I, Poles who were not yet American citizens volunteered in the tens of thousands to serve in the Polish Army that trained in Canada before going to Europe under Gen. Jozef Haller to fight for the Allied cause. When the United States entered the war in 1917, Polish Americans volunteered for service in the American Army in large numbers. By the end of the war, approximately 215,000 Polish Americans served in the U.S. armed forces, far beyond their relative proportion in the population. Those who did not serve in uniform also contributed generously. Records indicate that Poles in America, most of whom at that time held low-paying unskilled industrial jobs, purchased an astounding $67 million in American Liberty Bonds, with another $1.5 million raised specifically for the support of the Polish Army in France.

In the years of the economic growth during the 1920s and the Great Depression of the 1930s, Polish Americans rose to prominence in many fields of endeavor, not the least of which was the entertainment industry. A Shakespearean actress Helena Modjeska had already become popular on the American stage, to be followed by a host of operatic luminaries including Marcella Sembrich-Kochanska, Adam Didur, Jan Kiepura and the brothers Jan and Edouard de Reszke. Poles also made an immediate impact on the new medium of motion pictures, with Pola Negri filling early roles as the femme fatale in silent motion pictures. Gilda Gray gained fame as the "shimmy queen" of early movies, while Gloria Swanson, the daughter of a Polish mother in Chicago, became one of the leading screen actresses of her day. The ranks of producers and directors included Academy Award winning Joseph L. Mankiewicz who is best known for *All About Eve* and *The Philadelphia Story*. Samuel Goldwyn, a native of Warsaw, won Academy Awards as a producer and director, as well as established the famous "Leo the Lion" trademark that would later identify Metro-Goldwyn-Mayer productions. The famous Warner Brothers—Harry, Albert, Sam and Jack—migrated to the United States from Poland to establish Warner Brothers in 1918, the third oldest movie production company in the United States. These pioneers in the entertainment industry would be followed by a long line of stars from Carol Baker, Carole Landis and Stanley Andrews to Ted Knight, Stephanie Powers and Loretta Swit. Polish American contributions to the television and motion picture industries would fill more than one book.

Polish Americans also contributed to American culture through their musical talents. Gene Krupa redefined the role of the drums, as well as influencing the future of jazz and big band music, while flamboyant pianist Liberace, who studied with Paderewski, popularized the piano to millions of Americans. Conductors Artur Rodzinski and Leopold Stokowski led several orchestras to fame and popularity. Song writer Bronislaw Kaper authored the popular *Hi Lili, Hi Lo*, one of many Polish Americans to pen hit songs. And Bobby Vinton, the "Polish Prince", was the first to use Polish lyrics in a hit song, *My Melody of Love*.

The coming of the Second World War again brought Polish Americans into the armed forces in large numbers, as well as providing an opportunity for civilians to also demonstrate their patriotism. Author W. S. Kuniczak asserted that fully 12 percent of the U.S. armed forces during World War II were Polish Americans. Among those who distinguished themselves in uniform were Francis Gabreski, the highest scoring U.S. fighter ace in Europe and one of a handful of men to become aces in both propeller and jet aircrafts. Matthew Urban became the most decorated U.S. soldier of World War II, while the heroic efforts of several Polish Americans were recognized with the Medal of Honor. Among those who contributed as civilians were Stanislaw Ulam and Emil Konopinski, scientists essential to the Manhattan Project which developed the atomic bomb that finally ended the war. On the home front, the Polish National Alliance and the Polish Roman Catholic Union, the two largest Polish fraternal organizations in America, purchased enough U.S. bonds to pay for the production of five bombers, all of which were christened with Polish names. Virtually every Polish American community of any size organized to collect donations to aid Polish refugees and to support U.S. government drives to collect metal, used cooking oil, canned goods, and other products useful for the war effort.

The war also brought to the United States many refugees who would blend their talents with Polish Americans born in the U.S. to further the arts and sciences. These included scholars with international reputation, such as historian Jan Kucharzewski, literary scholar Waclaw Lednicki, jurist Rafal Taubenschlag, chemist Wojciech Swietoslawski and sociologist Feliks Gross. Alfred Korzybski originated the science of general semantics, Kazimierz Funk is credited with discovering vitamins, and Bronislaw

Malinowski, a leader in the study of ethnography, is widely considered to be one of the most influential anthropologists of the twentieth century. Jacob Bronowski created the immensely popular series *The Ascent of Man* (1973), which Carl Sagan later credited as his inspiration for *Cosmos* (1980).

The field of American literature was greatly enhanced by the novels of Monica Krawczyk whose short stories appeared in prominent publications such as the *Surveyor, Woman's Day, Good Housekeeping*, and the *Journal of National Education*. Jerzy Kosinski enjoyed great success with *The Painted Bird, Steps, Being There* and other novels, many focusing on life in the Soviet Union and the experiences of Poles under Nazi and Soviet rule. W. S. Kuniczak also wrote about experiences in World War II Poland in his trilogy, consisting of: *The Thousand Hour Day, The March* and *Valedictory*, after which he undertook a massive translation of Henryk Sienkiewicz's trilogy on Polish history, a work critics described as "masterful." Perhaps the most famous Polish literary figure to enrich America with his talents in recent years was the Nobel laureate poet Czeslaw Milosz, author of *The Captive Mind*, often considered the finest treatment of psychological response to oppressive government.

Another group that has left a lasting legacy in America is Polish American athletes. Oscar Bielaski became the first known Polish American professional baseball player throughout the nation and gained election to the elite circle of athletes enshrined in the various Halls of Fame. Their names read like a "who's who" of sports celebrities: Stan "The Man" Musial, Carl "Yaz" Yastrzemski, Al Simmons, Bill Mazeroski, Phil Niekro, Stanley Coveleski, Hank Stram, Jim Grabowski, Vic Janowicz, Stanley Ketchel, Mike Krzyzewski, Tony Kubek, Tara Lipinski, Janet Lynn, Bob Toski, Tony Zale, Stella Walsh, Alex Wojciechowicz, and a host of others.

Over the last generation, Polish Americans have also made noteworthy contributions to politics and national defense. Among the political leaders who have shaped recent American history are U.S. Senators Edmund Muskie, Barbara Mikulski, and Charles Hagel and Representatives Roman Pucinski, Daniel Rostenkowski, Marcy Kaptur, and Clement Zablocki. Zbigniew Brzezinski served as National Security Advisor, a position in which he played a key role in negotiating the Camp David Accords that led to the lasting peace agreement between Israel and Egypt. Gen. Edward Rowny served as an arms control adviser and negotiator to five presidents (Richard Nixon, Gerald Ford, Jimmy Carter, Ronald Reagan and George H. W. Bush), including negotiations leading to the SALT (Strategic Arms Limitation Treaty) and START (Strategic Arms Reduction Treaty) agreements. Another major contribution to the U.S. armed forces was made by chemist Stephanie L. Kwolek who created Kevlar, the material used to make bullet-proof protection for military personnel and law enforcement agencies. Four Polish Americans have participated in the U.S. space program as astronauts (Scott E. Parazynski, James A. Pawelczyk, Karol J. Bobko, and Christopher J. Ferguson), while others have served vital functions as engineers, electricians and managers.

Although this brief survey barely scratches the surface of the many contributions made by Polish Americans to the development of the United States, it illustrates the lengthy history of Americans of Polish descent, the breadth of fields of endeavor in which they have made lasting contributions and their continuing influence in America today.

ICONS OF THE PAST

TADEUSZ KOSCIUSZKO (1746-1817)
Chief Military Engineer of the Revolutionary War
Founder of West Point

By the time Tadeusz Kosciuszko was born, his family had lost most of its gentry status and holdings. His father died when the boy was young, and the family struggled with modest means. Under the patronage of the powerful Czartoryski family, Kosciuszko was admitted to the Cadet School in Warsaw where he studied political and military sciences. Upon graduation with the rank of a captain, he journeyed to Paris where he continued his studies in art, engineering and military science. Returning to Poland after the first partition of his homeland, he found little opportunity for advancement or even employment, prompting him to return to Paris where he learnt that there was a demand for engineers in the American revolutionary army. He travelled across the Atlantic in the late summer of 1776, and arrived in Philadelphia where he was assigned to design fortifications for the defense of the river approaches to Philadelphia. Commissioned colonel of engineers by the Continental Congress on October 18, Kosciuszko's engineering talents were soon brought to the attention of Gen. Horatio Gates who offered him the position of chief engineer when the general was assigned to command of the northern army operating in upper New York State.

Kosciuszko's first assignment was to assess the defenses of Fort Ticonderoga which he correctly predicted could be rendered untenable if the British placed artillery on Sugar Loaf Hill (now Mt. Defiance). Following the American defeat there Kosciuszko assumed command of the rear guard, fighting such a successful delaying action that the British were held up for a critical month during which the Americans were able to reorganize and gain reinforcements. At the crucial Battle of Saratoga that followed, Gen. Gates credited the victory to Kosciuszko's skills at selecting and fortifying the American position. From Saratoga, Kosciuszko was assigned to design and oversee construction of the vital fortifications at West Point along the Hudson River, today the site of the U.S. Military Academy. His work there gained lavish praise from American, British and French engineers for his innovative approach.

With the completion of his work at West Point, Kosciuszko joined the army in the Carolinas, arriving in the wake of a serious American defeat. Serving under Gen. Nathanael Greene, Kosciuszko earned praise for his skills in preparing the escape of the army across the Dan River, placing that barrier between the retreating Americans and their pursuers. Throughout the remainder of the campaigns in the South, Greene continued to praise Kosciuszko's work as critical to his success.

In recognition of his services in the American Revolution, he was offered membership in the prestigious Society of the Cincinnati and awarded a brevet promotion to brigadier general. George Washington presented him with a personal gift of two pistols. In 1828 the cadets at West Point raised funds to erect a column to Kosciuszko's memory, atop which stands a statue of the Pole.

Congress granted him citizenship and approved the National Park status for the home he occupied in Philadelphia. Among the many public recognitions of him in America is a prominent statue in Lafayette Park, across from the White House in Washington, D.C. Most symbolic of his quest for liberty was the fact that he penned a will leaving his American estate for purchasing the freedom of slaves and educating them to become good citizens. Thomas Jefferson proclaimed him to be "as pure a son of liberty as I have ever known."

KAZIMIERZ PULASKI (1746-1779)
The Hero of the Two Nations
Father of the American Cavalry

Born into a landed gentry family in Winiary, Poland in 1746. Pulaski's parents sent him to Warsaw to pursue the best education their relatively prosperous economic circumstances could afford. After completing legal and military studies, he assumed a position in the court of the Duke of Courland, but returned to Warsaw when Russian troops arrived to bring Poland under the influence of the Czar. Soon he became actively engaged in the Confederation of Bar, a revolutionary movement formed in 1768 by his father Joseph with a view to freeing Poland from Russian control. Quickly gaining a reputation for shrewd and tenacious military ability, he led forces in several campaigns against the Russians, defeating troops under the leadership of the famous Marshal Suvorov. His heroic and successful defense of Czestochowa in 1771 against the superior strength of the enemy has been immortalized in Jozef Chelmonski's famous painting *Pulaski at Czestochowa*. After the Confederation's defeat, Pulaski fled his homeland to Turkey, eventually making his way to France. Pulaski arrived in Paris where he met Benjamin Franklin, the emissary of the American revolutionary government to France. In his letter of introduction, Franklin described him as "an officer famous throughout Europe for his bravery and conduct in defense of the liberties of his country."

Upon his arrival in America, Pulaski initially served as a volunteer on the staff of General George Washington until the Continental Congress approved his commission. In this capacity, at the Battle of Brandywine he was credited with leading a cavalry force against an attempt by the British to outflank Washington's army, thereby giving the commanding general time to withdraw his forces in safety.

Following Brandywine, Congress confirmed Pulaski as a brigadier general and "Commander of the Horse," making him the ranking officer in charge of all cavalry. Often known as the "Father of the American Cavalry," he instituted a regular training routine that brought discipline and purpose to the American cavalry. After leading his force in several campaigns, Pulaski encountered difficulties with some American officers that prompted him to resign his position. Nevertheless, he remained in America to raise the independent Pulaski Legion organized along European lines as a joint force of cavalry and infantry. The Legion's flag was crafted by the Moravian Nuns in Bethlehem, Pennsylvania, as immortalized in Henry Wadsworth Longfellow's poem *Hymn of the Moravian Nuns*.

Sent south to oppose British operations in the Carolinas, Pulaski and his troops successfully defended Charleston, South Carolina, and then participated in the joint Franco-American attack on Savannah where he was mortally wounded while rallying the troops to charge the British entrenchments. As a hero of the American Revolution, his name has been taken by numerous cities and counties throughout the country, Fort Pulaski in Savannah was named in his honor, and his statue can be found in various cities including Freedom Plaza in Washington, D.C. By presidential proclamation, October 11 is reserved each year for the commemoration of Pulaski Day. In the State of Illinois Kazimierz Pulaski Day is a holiday observed on the first Monday of every March.

CHRISTIAN BREVOORT ZABRISKIE (1864-1936)
The Man who Has His Point in Death Valley

One of the first Polish settlers to arrive in North America was Olbracht Zaborowski who immigrated to the Dutch colony of New Amsterdam in 1662. Once there, he learned the local Indian language, served as an interpreter, and became a wealthy landowner with title to much of what is today northern New Jersey. Throughout the generations, his offspring, with their name changed to Zabriskie, took prominent parts in the westward movement, the American Civil War and other events that shaped American history. One of his descendants, Christian Brevoort Zabriskie, came into the world at Fort Bridger in the Wyoming Territory on October 16, 1864.

Zabriskie learned the trade of a telegrapher quite early, taking his first job as a telegraph operator with the Virginia & Truckee railroad in Carson City, Nevada. Later he moved to Candelaria to accept a position with the Esmeralda County Bank. In 1885 Francis M. "Borax" Smith hired Zabriskie as a manager in his Harmony Borax Works located nearby and in 20 Mule Team Canyon. In 1890 Smith bought out the holdings of a rival company, consolidating them with his own under the name Pacific Coast Borax Company. Zabriskie rose rapidly through the ranks of the company, eventually being named vice president and general manager, positions he held for thirty-six years.

During his tenure, the company prospered, its "20-Mule Team Borax" slogan becoming a household word. The slogan and the product gained much popular recognition as the sponsor of the popular television program *Death Valley Days* first hosted by the "Old Ranger" played by Polish-American actor Stanley Andrews (Stanislaw Andrzejewski).

Zabriskie Point, a popular tourist spot located in the Amargosa Mountains within the Death Valley National Park, is named after him. From its summit one can view the rugged scenery of Gold Canyon, Telescope Peak, Manly Beacon and other spectacular sites whose gold color derives from the high concentration of borax that originally drew the company to the area. Zabriskie retired in 1933, the same year the National Park was established.

FATHER JOSEPH DABROWSKI (?-1903)
Founder of Saints Cyril and Methodius Seminary

One of the most important aspects of their cultural heritage that ethnic Poles brought to the United States was the Roman Catholic faith. They relied on their faith to see them through the difficult transition to a new culture with an unfamiliar language, and they based the beginning of their lives in America on the construction of churches to serve as centers for community development. To minister to these settlements, many priests migrated from Poland, among them Father Joseph Dabrowski. A participant in the unsuccessful Polish January Insurrection against the Russians, he fled Poland to Switzerland and further to Rome where he joined the Resurrectionists and was ordained in 1869. The following year he left for the United States and went to St. Francis Seminary near Milwaukee, Wisconsin. Appointed the pastor at Polonia, Wisconsin, he urged the Resurrectionist Order in Rome to send additional Polish priests to educate the Poles in America, and was responsible for the establishment of the Resurrectionist missionaries among the scattered Polish rural settlements in America. In 1874 he sent a letter to Krakow, Poland and invited the Felician Sisters, a teaching order, to send sisters to open a school in Polonia. Five arrived later that year, the first representatives of a religious order that would become synonymous with parochial education in America. In 1876 the Felician Sisters in Poland formally established the Felician Province in America, quickly becoming the largest teaching order serving the Polish minority. To support their teaching efforts, Dabrowski bought a printing press where he published textbooks, primers, catechisms, almanacs, and other items designed to promote Polish history and culture.

In 1882 Dabrowski moved to Detroit, Michigan, where, with the assistance of Father Leopold Moczygeba, he established Saints Cyril and Methodius Seminary, the first Polish seminary in the United States. The new institution was blessed in 1885, and it opened its doors two years later. Father Dabrowski served as its head for nineteen years, providing leadership for an institution that later expanded to include a high school and St. Mary's College. Over the years, the seminary educated hundreds of young Polish Americans for service to their communities. In 1909 the seminary moved to nearby Orchard Lake, where it operates until today.

HELENA MODJESKA (1840-1909)
Legendary Shakespearean Actress

Born in Krakow, Poland in 1840, Helena Modrzejewska was the daughter of the celebrated musician Michal Opid. Pursuing an early interest in the theater, she rose to prominence on the stage in her native city in the early 1860s. After her husband Gustaw Modrzejewski died in 1861, she married Count Karol Bozenta Chlapowski but kept her original stage name of Modrzejewska. With Chlapowski's support, she moved to Warsaw where she accepted an engagement with the renowned Warsaw Theater. There she gained critical acclaim as a Shakespearean actress, her most famous role probably being that of Ophelia in *Hamlet*. In 1876 the couple moved to the United States, settling in a Polish utopian community on a ranch in California that she purchased. Located in what today is Anaheim, the colony attracted intellectuals such as Julian Sypniewski and future Nobel laureate Henrk Sienkiewicz. Changing her name to "Modjeska" to make it easier for English-speaking audiences to pronounce, she began her American career in San Francisco in 1877 in the title role in *Adrienne Lecouveur*, a performance arranged largely by the Polish community resident in San Francisco, and especially through the support of Gen. Wlodzimierz Krzyzanowski. Throughout a lengthy career that stretched into the first decade of the twentieth century, she played twelve different Shakespearean roles including Ophelia *(Hamlet)*, Juliet *(Romeo and Juliet)*, Desdemona *(Othello)*, and Queen Anne *(Richard III)*, becoming widely recognized as the foremost Shakespearean actress of her day. She also starred as Marguerite Gautier in *Camille* and the title roles in Victor Hugo's *Tisbé* and Schiller's *Maria Stuart* and *Princess Eboli*. She is also credited with introducing the work of Henrik Ibsen to the United States by staging his *A Doll's House* in 1883.

Modjeska was well-received on tours of England in 1880, 1881 and 1885, and also visited Poland frequently, playing roles in Krakow, Lodz, Lublin, Lvov, Poznan, Stanislawowo, Tarnow and Warsaw. On May 2, 1905 she gave a jubilee performance in New York City. Then she toured for two years and ended her acting career, afterward only appearing sporadically in support of charitable causes.

Modjeska died at Newport Beach, California on April 8, 1909, aged 68, from undisclosed causes. Her remains were sent to Krakow to be buried in the family grave at the Rakowiecki Cemetery.

Her son Ralph Modjeski, was a noted engineer who gained a national reputation in the United States for his work on various bridge projects. Her home *Arden* in Modjeska Canyon, California, is on the register of National Historic Landmarks. The theater in the old town of Krakow, her native city, is named in her honor.

RALPH MODJESKI (1861-1940)
America's Greatest Bridge Builder

Ralph Modjeski was born near the city of Krakow, Poland on January 27, 1861. He immigrated to America at the age of 15 with his mother, famous Shakespearean actress, Helena Modjeska, in July 1876.

Even though Modjeski seemed to become an accomplished concert pianist, he directed his considerable talents to engineering. After graduating with a degree in civil engineering from the celebrated *l'Ecole des Ponts et Chaussees* in Paris in 1885, he returned to the United States where he set up Modjeski & Noble, a company specializing in the construction of bridges.

His first project as a lead engineer was the construction of railroad bridges across the Mississippi River Rock Island, Illinois. He served for a while as a consulting engineer for the city of Chicago, but gained his reputation primarily from the construction of bridges including the Bismarck Bridge for the Northern Pacific Railroad; the Columbia and Willamette River Bridges for the Portland & Seattle Railway; the McKinley Bridge at St. Louis; the Broadway Bridge in Portland, Oregon; the Columbia River Bridge in Cecilo, Oregon; the Cherry Street Bridge in Toledo, Ohio; the Memphis Bridge in Tennessee; the Delaware River Bridge (later re-named the Benjamin Franklin Bridge) between Philadelphia and Camden, New Jersey; the Tacony-Palmyra Bridge over the Delaware River in Northeast Philadelphia; the Mid-Hudson Bridge in New York State; the New Orleans Bridge and the Huey P. Long Bridge in New Orleans; the Thebes Bridge over the Mississippi River at Thebes, Illinois; the Iowa-Illinois Memorial Bridge at Davenport; the Calvert Street Bridge in Washington, D.C.; the Trans-Bay Bridge between San Francisco and Oakland in California; and the Blue Water Bridge connecting Port Huron, Michigan, and Sarnia, Ontario, Canada. Among his more important works was re-designing a poorly conceived Quebec Bridge in 1907, a project that is still the longest cantilever bridge in the world.

Labeled by the *New York Times* as "the world's leading bridge builder," he was honored with the John Scott Medal in Philadelphia (1924); the John Fritz Medal (1930), the most prestigious engineering award in America; the Washington Award (1931); the Grand Prix Medal of the Exposition of Industry and Science in Poznan, Poland (1929); and Knight of the Legion of Honor from France. He also received honorary doctoral degrees from the Pennsylvania Military College (1927; now Widener University) and the Polytechnic University in Lvov (1931).

JOSEPH KARGÉ (1823-1892)
Civil War Brigadier General

Throughout the nineteenth century, Poles gained a reputation for their persistent pursuit of freedom, whether in the cause of their own nation or that of others. One of these international freedom fighters was Joseph Karge who fought in the 1848 revolution, the "Springtime of Nations." Born near Poznan in 1823, he attended local schools until enrolling in the University in Wroclaw to pursue studies in history and linguistics. Following the unsuccessful revolutions of 1848, Karge was condemned to death *in absentia* for his participation, necessitating his escape to France. From there he continued his flight to England and then to the United States, arriving in New York in 1851.

From the time of his arrival in the United States until the outbreak of the Civil War, Karge taught languages and classics in New York. With the beginning of the war, he obtained a commission as lieutenant colonel in the 1st New Jersey Cavalry, rising quickly to the rank of a colonel in a regiment that he developed into a well-trained unit with a fine reputation for discipline and fighting spirit. Wounded in 1862 during the campaign leading up to the Battle of Second Bull Run, he returned to duty in about four weeks, in time to participate in the Fredericksburg Campaign. The active campaign, however, aggravated the wound which had not yet healed and he was forced for medical reasons to resign his commission before the end of the year.

Recovered from his wound after several months, Karge obtained approval to recruit the 2nd New Jersey Cavalry. The regiment was assigned to Army of the Tennessee in November, 1863. By April of 1864, Karge had risen to command of a brigade of cavalry which he led during Gen. William T. Sherman's campaign to capture Atlanta. Karge also participated in Gen. Benjamin H. Grierson's raids into Tennessee and Alabama. One of the highpoints of his service came when he commanded the Union forces that defeated the noted Confederate Gen. Nathan Bedford Forest at Bolivar, Tennessee. For his service, Karge was promoted to a brigadier general in April 1865.

Following the war, Karge served in the U.S. Army for several years before accepting a position as chair of the Department of Languages and Literature at Princeton College (later Princeton University), a position he held until his death over twenty years later.

WLODZIMIERZ KRZYZANOWSKI (1824-1887)
Civil War Brigadier General

Krzyzanowski grew up in a family rich in Polish patriotism. His father fought with Napoleon in the vain hope of resurrecting Polish independence, while his older brother joined the November Uprising of 1830-31. His sister married Fryderyk Chopin, whose talents added greatly to Polish national and cultural heritage. With these values instilled in him from childhood, it is little wonder that he joined a group of conspirators planning another Polish revolt under Ludwik Mieroslawski in 1846. The plot failed, he escaped a court sentence by fleeing west. Eventually he arrived in New York City.

After participating in an ill-fated attempt to found a Polish colony in western Virginia (today West Virginia), he settled in Washington, D.C., where he married, began operating a pottery store, and gained a reputation as an effective speaker in the local immigrant political circles. At the outbreak of the Civil War, he immediately joined the Washington militia where he was assigned to guard the capital until federal troops arrived. After raising Company B, the "Turner Rifles," for the D. C. militia, of which he became captain, he obtained authority from the War Department to organize a regiment. Moving his recruiting efforts to more populous New York City, he succeeded in recruiting the 58th New York Volunteer Infantry, largely from the city's immigrant communities, which later came to be known as the "Polish Legion." Krzyzanowski's regiment saw its first action at the Battle of Cross Keys on June 8, 1862, gaining praise from witnesses for its steadfastness in protecting a federal artillery battery. Following the engagement, with the reorganization of the Union forces, Krzyzanowski was placed in command of the 2nd Brigade, 3rd Division, First Corps, of the Army of Virginia after which the federal armies in the East were consolidated, with Krzyzanowski receiving command of the 2nd Brigade, 3rd Division, Eleventh Corps, Army of the Potomac. Caught up in the Union disaster at Chancellorsville in May of 1863, Krzyzanowski again earned praise in a losing effort for standing firm against overwhelming Confederate assaults. At Gettysburg in July 1863, when Confederate forces captured a position in the center of the Union line, threatening yet another defeat, Krzyzanowski led a successful counterattack that repulsed the Confederate attack. Moving west, he participated in relieving the sieges of Chattanooga and Nashville before being assigned to command troops protecting an important supply line furnishing Gen. William Tecumseh Sherman's army as it moved to capture Atlanta.

Following the war, Krzyzanowski served in a number of posts including an agent of the U. S. Treasury in Georgia, Alabama, Florida, Louisiana, the Washington Territory, Panama, and New York City. Retiring briefly to San Francisco in the 1870s, he was instrumental in arranging the American debut of the noted Polish actress Helena Modjeska (Modrzejewska), as well as operating a tavern frequented by novelist Henryk Sienkiewicz. It was at Krzyzanowski tavern where Sienkiewicz met many of the personalities that he would later develop into characters in his novels.

For his services during the war, he was promoted to the brevet rank of brigadier general in 1865. Originally buried in Greenwood Cemetery in New York, his remains, and those of his wife, were transferred to Arlington National Cemetery on the fiftieth anniversary of his death in 1937.

JAN HENRYK DE ROSEN
(1891-1982)
Master of the Mural

Born in Warsaw in 1891, de Rosen inherited a love of fine arts from his father, a noted artist for the Czarist courts of Alexander II and Nicholas II. After serving in the French and Polish armies during World War I, where he was recognized with both French and Polish decorations, he acted as an attaché and translator to Ignacy Jan Paderewski at the Versailles Peace Conference before returning to Poland. In 1937 he journeyed to the United States at the invitation of the Polish ambassador to Washington, Count Jerzy Potocki. With the German invasion of Poland in 1939, de Rosen could not return home so he worked at the Polish Embassy painting a mural titled *A Glory of the Polish Army.* The painting was covered by the authorities in 1948 because the images in it incorporated symbols and ideas which were not in line with the ideology of the communist government. Only towards the end of the 1980's the painting was "rediscovered", renovated in Warsaw, and returned to its place at the Embassy, where it still can be viewed by the visitors. Subsequently Rosen took a position teaching liturgical art at The Catholic University of America. For his wartime services to the Polish Government-in-Exile, he was awarded Polish, French and British decorations.

De Rosen pursued the remainder of his career in the United States, completing work on the Chapel of the Nativity's Adoration in 1946 and executing his critically acclaimed mosaic "Christ in Majesty" at the Basilica of the National Shrine of the Immaculate Conception adjacent to the Catholic University campus in Washington D.C. At 3,600 square feet and containing nearly 3 million tiles, "Christ in Majesty" is one of the largest mosaics of Jesus in the world. His other works include the mosaic on the dome of the Catholic Cathedral in St. Louis, as well as other works in Buffalo, Memphis, San Francisco, St. Louis and Pittsburgh. One of his more extensive projects was undertaken at Grace Cathedral where he fashioned eight separate wax tempura murals and seven aisle panels. These works illustrate figures and events from Christian and English traditions including St. Augustine, Father Junipero Serra, St. Francis, King Ethelbert and Francis Drake. Two of his murals are in the collections of the papal summer residence at Castel Gandolfo in Italy.

Among his many honors, on the recommendation of Polish Cardinal Stefan Wyszynski, Pope Paul VI inducted de Rosen into the Order of St. Gregory the Great, a papal award established by Pope Gregory XVI in 1831 to honor distinguished contributions. The American Council for Polish Culture offers in his honor the Jan de Rosen Award for artistic achievement.

MIECZYSLAW G. BEKKER (1905-1989)
Constructor of the Lunar Rover

Like so many scientists, mathematicians and humanists, Mieczyslaw Bekker dreamt of a career in his native Poland. Born near Hrubieszow on the eastern edge of Poland in 1905, he earned a degree from Warsaw Technical University in 1929 and accepted a position at Army Engineering Research Institute in Warsaw specializing in studies to improve the mobility of tracked vehicles across uneven terrain. The German and Soviet invasion of 1939 put an end to what he had hoped would be a long and fruitful career in the service of his country. When his military unit was forced to retreat into Romania, he fled to France, and with the fall of France in 1940 escaped to England. Two years later he accepted an offer to continue his work on armored vehicles for the Canadian government, rising to the rank of lieutenant colonel in the Canadian Army. When his service ended in 1956, he moved to the United States.

While serving as assistant professor of engineering at the University of Michigan, he also conducted work on tracked vehicles for the U.S. Army before accepting a position at General Motors in 1961 that provided him with an opportunity to work on the development of a projected vehicle for traveling on the surface of the Moon. For his contributions to the project, he is generally considered to be the father of the Lunar Rover employed on the Apollo 15, 16 and 17 missions to the Moon. During each of the three missions the astronauts made a few trips using the LRV and travelling on the Moon surface with the maximum speed of 11 mph. All three LRVs remained on the Moon.

Regarded as a foremost specialist in the development of military and other off-road vehicles, Bekker is the founder of the new engineering discipline known as "terramechanics". He holds a number of patents and is the author of a pioneering book on vehicle design, *Theory of Land Locomotion* (University of Michigan Press, 1956) and a subsequent book *Off-the-Road Locomotion* (University of Michigan Press, 1960). His third work, *Introduction to Terrain Vehicle Systems* (University of Michigan Press, 1969) included much of his initial research on the Lunar Roving Vehicle design. He has been recognized for his achievements with the Golden Columbus Medal from the city of Genoa, Italy, and with honorary doctorates from Munich University of Technology, the University of Ottawa and the University of Bologna.

KAZIMIERZ FUNK (1884-1967)
Discoverer of Vitamins

Born in Warsaw in 1884, Kazimierz (Casimir) Funk acquired from his physician father a love of science and scientific inquiry. After earning his doctorate in organic chemistry at the University of Bern in Switzerland in 1904, Funk pursued research first at the Pasteur Institute in Paris, then the Wiesbaden Municipal Hospital, the University of Berlin, and the Lister Institute for Preventative Medicine in London. In England in 1912 he first published the idea that led him to the discovery of what he labeled "vitamines." His original discovery subsequently became known as Thiamine, or Vitamin B1. Since his initial work was focused on finding a remedy for beriberi, a disorder of the nervous system, Funk later advanced the theory that other maladies such as pellagra, rickets and scurvy could also be cured through the use of appropriate vitamins. He also theorized and then confirmed the existence of Vitamins B2, C and D, and is credited with being the first scientist to isolate Niacin, or Vitamin B3. He published his first book *The Vitamine* (1913) based on this early research. In 1913 he became head of biochemistry at the Cancer Hospital Research Institute in London.

Funk moved to the United States in 1915 to accept a position with Cornell Medical College. In 1921 he joined H. A. Metz and Company where he developed a Vitamin A and D concentrate called Oscosol, as well as Salvarsan used in the treatment of syphilis. Returning to Poland in 1923 he accepted a position as head of the biochemistry program at the National Institute for Hygiene in Warsaw. There he conducted important research on the isolation of insulin and the affect of vitamin B1 on the metabolism of carbohydrates. In 1928 he moved to Paris as a consultant to the Casa Biochemica research institute. The onset of World War II forced him to flee to the United States in 1939 where he founded the Funk Foundation for Medical Research (1940). He is also noted for his research on hormones, diabetes, ulcers and cancer. He died in Albany, New York at the age of 82.

The Polish Institute of Arts & Sciences in America offers the Casimir Funk Natural Sciences Award in his honor.

FRANCIS GABRESKI (1919-2002)
Flying Ace

Born in Oil City, Pennsylvania in 1919, "Gabby" Gabreski spent two years at the University of Notre Dame where he took six hours of flying lessons that sparked in him a great interest, leading him to enroll in the U.S. Army Air Corps in 1938. Although he struggled to complete the courses of instruction, he finally earned his wings and a commission of second lieutenant in March 1941. Assigned to Wheeler Field in Hawaii, he was there when the Japanese attacked on December 7, 1941. Since he spoke Polish, in September 1942 he was assigned as liaison officer to the Polish squadrons operating with the British Royal Air Force in England. In this role, he flew Spitfires on some twenty combat missions with the Polish 315th "Deblinski" Squadron. In February 1943 Gabreski joined the 61st U.S. Fighter Squadron. Flying the P-47 Thunderbolt, he soon rose to flight and then squadron command. With the 61st, he shot down his first German aircraft, an FW-190, over France in August 1943. By the end of November he was credited with five "kills," making him an "ace." Over the next few months his "score" rose steadily. In the spring of 1944 he surpassed the total reached by America's leading ace in World War I, Eddie Rickenbacker, and in July 1944 became the leading U.S. ace with 28 kills to his credit, a total that ranked him as the leading U.S. fighter pilot in Europe during the entire war. Following the war, Gabreski worked for Douglas Aircraft and earned a Bachelor of Science degree in political science from Columbia University. Recalled to active duty, he flew the F-86 jet fighter in Korea where he shot down a 6.5 MIG fighters, making him one of only seven pilots to become aces in both propeller and jet aircrafts. Following the Korean War, Gabreski remained in the service for another fifteen years commanding various units. After his retirement he worked for Grumman Aerospace, as well as serving a brief term as president of the Long Island Railroad.

During his exceptional career he was awarded the Distinguished Service Cross, Distinguished Service Medal, two Silver Stars, the Legion of Merit, a remarkable thirteen Distinguished Flying Crosses, a Bronze Star, and five Air Medals. He also received the Distinguished Flying Cross of the United Kingdom, the French Croix de Guerre with Palm, the French Legion of Honor, the Belgian Crois de Guerre and the Polish Krzyz Walecznych. In 1978 he was elected to the National Aviation Hall of Fame, and in 1991 the Suffolk County Airport near New York City was renamed Francis S. Gabreski Airport in his honor.

JOHN GRONOUSKI (1919-1996)
Postmaster General who Introduced Zip Codes

A native of Dunbar, Wisconsin, John Gronouski was the grandson of Franciszek Gronowski who immigrated to the United States from western Poland in 1875. He grew up in a Polish-American community, an experience he valued for the rest of his life. During World War II, Gronouski served as a navigator on 24 combat missions with the Eighth Air Force in Europe. He earned his bachelor's, master's and doctoral degrees from the University of Wisconsin before accepting employment with the Wisconsin Department of Taxation, rising to Commissioner of Taxation by 1960.

An ardent Democrat, he opposed the tactics of Senator Joseph McCarthy's "Red Scare", streamlined the tax system in the state, and provided what some scholars believe was a crucial state endorsement of John F. Kennedy during his bid for the presidency. With his election, President Kennedy nominated Gronouski Postmaster General, the first Polish-American to be appointed to a Cabinet position. He quickly became a favorite with the Washington press corps because of his openness and frankness. He also became an outspoken advocate for racial equality in postal employment, promoted the original five-digit zip code system, reorganizing the postal service to improve delivery, and instituting various cost-saving measures.

President Lyndon B. Johnson nominated Gronouski Ambassador to Poland in 1965. In that position, he served as somewhat of a "roving ambassador" to Eastern Europe, frequently visiting the Soviet Union and other Eastern Bloc nations in an effort to build economic and cultural ties. With the end of the Johnson administration, Gronouski became involved in the development of a curriculum in public policy and administration for the University of Texas, becoming the founding dean of the Lyndon B. Johnson School of Public Affairs. After stepping down as dean in 1974, he continued as a faculty member until 1989.

During the 1970s he served as a court-appointed head of Milwaukee's efforts to desegregate its public schools. In 1974 President Jimmy Carter named Gronouski Chairman of the Board for International Broadcasting, charged with operating both Radio Free Europe and Radio Liberty.

He spent the last years of his life in Green Bay, Wisconsin where he died on January 7, 1996.

JOZEF HOFMANN (1876-1957)
Virtuoso Pianist who Invented Windshield Wipers

This virtuoso pianist, composer, teacher and inventor was born on January 20, 1876 in Krakow in a very musical family. His father was a composer and pianist and his mother was a singer. Jozef started learning to play the piano at the age of three. When he was eight, he gave a concert in Warsaw during which he played a Mozart concerto. Two years later, Jozef had his first European tour playing in Germany, Denmark, Sweden, Holland, France, and England. Before long he came to America. His concert at the Metropolitan Opera House was such a huge success that he was offered a contract and within the following 10 weeks he played 52 concerts. Hailed as a child prodigy, he became a media celebrity. However, his American tour was stopped by the New York Society for the Prevention of Cruelty to Children which saw it as an example of child exploitation. Young Jozef was offered a scholarship of $ 50,000 by Alfred Corning Clark who wanted him to refrain from public concerts until he became 18. The money enabled Josef to study under the supervision of Moritz Moszkowski, a famous teacher and composer and Anton Rubinstein, a Russian virtuoso and composer. In 1894 Rubinstein arranged Hofmann's debut as a mature pianist in Hamburg, Germany. Hofmann played Rubinstein's Piano Concerto No. 4 in D minor with the composer on the podium. After the success of this concert, Hofmann started his virtuoso career again. He played in many countries of Europe and in the USA. He was exceptionally gifted with a phenomenal musical memory. Once Hofmann learned a piece of music, it stayed in his mind for good. Reportedly, he had the ability to hear a composition once and to play it back flawlessly without seeing the printed musical notation. In St. Petersburg he gave 21 consecutive concerts not repeating a single piece and playing the total of 255 different works. Hofmann made the United States his home during World War I. In 1926 he became an American citizen. From 1926 until 1938 he was director of the Curtis Institute of Music in Philadelphia. Hofmann also made a few commercial recordings of his performance, some of which were the earliest recordings of classical music for Thomas A. Edison. Recorded broadcasts of some of Hofmann's live performances have survived and have been published on compact discs.

In view of the artist's exceptionally small hands, Steinway made a special piano for him with narrower keys, which were more comfortable for him. The artist ended his piano career on January 19, 1946 with a concert at Carnegie Hall. He is recognized by many as one of the greatest pianists of the 20th century.

For an artist, Jozef Hofmann had an unusual interest in technology. His inventions include car pneumatic shock absorbers and windshield wipers. They earned him a fortune in the early years of the 20th c. It is said that the idea of windshield wipers came to him when he was staring at the pendulum of a metronome. Altogether he patented about 70 inventions. He devoted the last years of his life to improvements in piano recording. Jozef Hofmann died in Los Angeles on February 16, 1957.

JAN KARSKI (1914 - 2000)
The Man who Tried to Stop the Holocaust

Diplomat, soldier of the Polish underground army during World War II, professor at Georgetown University, the man who tried to stop the Holocaust.

Jan Karski was born as Jan Kozielewski in Lodz, Poland on June 24, 1914. From the earliest days of his childhood, he lived in a multi-cultural society, predominantly Jewish. Having finished a local high school, he went on to study Law and Diplomatic Science at Lvov University, where he graduated in 1935. He joined the Polish diplomatic corps and served at posts in Germany, Switzerland and Great Britain. After the outbreak of World War II he was arrested by the Soviet Red Army. By a stroke of luck, he escaped from the train heading for a POW camp and soon he joined the Polish underground movement. This is when he adopted the pseudonym of Jan Karski which later became his legal name. During one of his courier missions between Great Britain, France and Poland he was arrested in the mountains by the Gestapo. Severely tortured, he was transported to a hospital from where he was rescued by underground soldiers. In the summer of 1942 Karski was chosen to perform a special mission. He was to take information about the situation in Poland to Gen. Sikorski, Prime Minister of the Polish Government in Exile. In order to collect hard facts about the extermination of Jews, Karski was smuggled to the Warsaw Ghetto and to a Nazi German concentration camp in occupied Eastern Poland. Risking his life he learnt the truth about the Jewish extermination. What he saw there was so atrocious that he was never able to talk about it calmly. In the fall of 1942 he set off on the most important journey of his life. Via France, Portugal and Gibraltar he came to Great Britain where he met members of the Polish Government in Exile to whom he reported all he had witnessed in Poland. He also met leaders of the British government as well as writers and journalists to tell them his story. He continued his mission by going to the United States, where on July 28, 1943 his famous meeting with President Roosevelt took place at the White House. As he had promised to the Jews who showed him around the Warsaw Ghetto, he told their story to the most powerful man of the free world, informing him that 1.8 million Jews had already been killed and that failure to intervene on the part of the Allies would bring destruction to the Jews of Poland. However, the American leaders and politicians, including President Roosevelt, did not believe his horrifying stories.

Karski could not return to Poland because the Germans had found out his identity. He was ordered to stay in the United States. In 1944 he wrote a book titled *Story of a Secret State* which once again described his experience in Poland under the German occupation. The Yalta agreement put Poland at the wrong side of the "Iron Curtain", so Karski could not return there again. He became an exile and for years he remained largely forgotten. He obtained a PhD degree from Georgetown University in 1952, two years later became an American citizen, and in 1965 he married a dancer and choreographer Pola Nirenska. He continued to teach at Georgetown University for 40 years. Among his students was the future 42nd President of the

United States - Bill Clinton. As a delegate of the U.S. Department of State, Karski lectured in many countries of the world. His participation in the film *Shoah* in 1978 reintroduced him to the world as the man who tried to stop the Holocaust. His popularity grew enormously. In 1982 he was named "the Righteous among Nations," in 1994 he became an honorary citizen of the State of Israel. He received the Order of the White Eagle (the highest Polish civil decoration) as well as the Order of Virtuti Militari (the highest Polish military decoration). In 1998 he was nominated for the Nobel Peace Prize.

Karski died in Washington on July 13, 2000, but his legend lives on. He was honored with special monuments - the Karski benches, depicting him sitting on a bench playing his favorite game of chess, which have already been erected at Georgetown University Campus in Washington D.C., in front of the Consulate General of Poland in New York and in the city of Kielce, Poland.

JAN KIEPURA (1902-1966)
The Heartthrob of the Opera

Tenor and actor, one of the most famous opera singers and actors of the inter war period.

"A boy from Sosnowiec" (a city in Poland) - as he called himself, was born there in a baker's family on May 16, 1902. Having graduated from high school and wanting to fulfill his father's wish, he went to Warsaw to study law at Warsaw University. During his studies he began taking singing lessons, keeping it secret from his parents. Soon he was admitted to Warsaw Opera where he debuted in 1924, singing a small part in the Polish national opera *Halka* by Stanislaw Moniuszko. His real stage debut came the following year when on February 11 he performed the title role in Gounod's *Faust*, shortly followed by performances in *Rigolletto*, *Tosca*, *Halka* (main part) and *Haunted Manor*. Dreaming of a world career, Kiepura decided to leave Warsaw for Vienna where he impressed the director of the Vienna Staatsoper so much that he offered him a role in *Tosca* in September of 1926. Then came the engagements in Berlin, London, and finally in the legendary La Scala in Milan where he sang for the first time in *Turandot* on January 19, 1928. He continued his opera career singing in Buenos Aires and Rio de Janeiro as well as Paris, Copenhagen, Berlin and other European cities. At the same time, Kiepura started his movie career which made him even more popular. His films include *City of Song*, *Give Us This Night*, *The Charm of La Boheme*, and *The Land of Smiles*. In 1934 while shooting *My Heart is Calling* Kiepura met a Hungarian singer and actress Martha Eggerth, whom he married in 1936.

On January 10, 1938 he debuted at the Metropolitan Opera as Rudolfo in Pucinni's *La Boheme*, where he sang until 1942 in *Tosca*, *Carmen* and *Rigoletto*. In the meantime, Kiepura produced *The Marry Widow* on Broadway in which he appeared with his wife Martha Eggerth. It was such an outstanding success that they toured the United States and then Europe singing it in four languages.

Whenever Kiepura returned to Poland he was given a hero's welcome by the crowds. He sang for his audience not only on stage but from car roofs, hotel balconies or windows of train carriages.

He died of a heart attack in his mansion in Harrison near New York City on August 15, 1966. As he so wished, he was buried in Warsaw on September 3, 1966. Thousands of people paid homage to the coffin in the lobby of *The Grand Theatre* before it was buried at *Powazki* - the most famous cemetery in Warsaw.

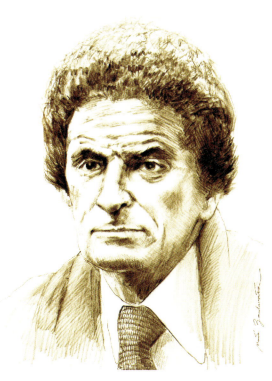

JERZY KOSINSKI (1933-1991)
The Painted Bird

Josek Lewinkopf was born into the Jewish community in Lodz, Poland in 1933. He survived World War II thanks to a Catholic family that sheltered him using a forged baptismal certificate in the name of Jerzy Kosinski given to him by a Catholic priest. Following the war, he studied history and political science at the University of Lodz before migrating to the United States in 1957. Settling first in New York, he earned a degree from Columbia University, he then taught at Yale, Princeton, Davenport University and Wesleyan.

Kosinski's first two novels, *The Future Is Ours, Comrade* (1960) and *No Third Path* (1962), published under the pseudonym of Joseph Novak, explored anticommunist themes. His literary reputation bloomed with the publication, under his own name, of *The Painted Bird* (1965) - somewhat controversial novel depicting the horrors and brutality of World War II as seen through the eyes of a boy of unknown religious and ethnic background wandering about a surreal Central or Eastern Europe countryside and hiding among cruel peasants. His second novel, *Steps* (1968), a series of literary vignettes, was recognized with the National Book Award in 1969. His next novel, *Being There* (1971) was turned into a movie in 1979 starring Peter Sellers. Directed by Hal Ashby, Kosinski co-authored the screenplay version with Robert C. Jones. The movie version of the novel received the Best Screenplay Award from the British Academy of Film and Television Arts, the award for Best Comedy Adapted from Another Medium from the Writers Guild of America, and was nominated for a Golden Globe for Best Screenplay. His other works included *The Devil Tree* (1973), *Cockpit* (1975), *Blind Date* (1977), *Passion Play* (1978), *Pinball* (1982), *The Hermit of 69th Street* (1988), and *Passing By: Selected Essays, 1962-1991* (1992).

In 1973 Kosinski was elected President of American P.E.N. - the New York based chapter of this international organization for poets, playwrights, essayists, editors, and novelists. A popular guest on the talk show circuit, Kosinski made twelve appearances on *The Tonight Show Starring Johnny Carson* and *The Dick Cavett Show*. His other interests included photography - exhibitions of his photography were held in Warsaw in 1957 and the Andre Zarre Gallery in New York in 1988, as well as acting - he played the role of a Bolshevik Grigory Zinoviev in the film *Reds*.

RYSZARD KUKLINSKI (1930-2004)
Secret Life that Helped End the Cold War Era

Code name "Jack Strong" - a Polish officer and a C.I.A. spy who worked with the Americans for nine years and became one of the C.I.A.'s most important and most productive agents. Kuklinski was born in Warsaw in 1930 into a working class family. His father, a member of the Polish underground resistance movement during World War II, was arrested by the Gestapo and died in Sachsenhausen concentration camp. At 17, Ryszard joined the army of the communist Poland and embarked on a brilliant military career. He was promoted promptly and in 1968, already as a high ranking officer, took part in the preparations for the Warsaw Pact invasion on Czechoslovakia. Two years later he was outraged by the fact that the Polish authorities ordered the riot troops to fire at demonstrators in Gdansk, killing 47 of them. In 1972, while on a boating trip in Germany, he contacted the American Embassy in Bonn asking for a clandestine meeting.

Soon his life of an agent began when he met two C.I.A. case officers. Over the course of the next nine years Kuklinski covertly provided the United States with Soviet military secrets of every kind, including strategic plans of the Warsaw Pact, the distribution of Soviet anti-aircraft bases, technical data of their weapons etc. In December 1980, Kuklinski disclosed Soviet plans to invade Poland in order to suppress *Solidarity* - the first free trade union in the Soviet block. President Carter was able to warn the Soviets in time about the possible consequences of such an invasion and it never happened. The following year Kuklinski gave advance warning of Poland's plans to impose martial law. Altogether he is said to have handed over to the Americans about 40 thousand pages of documents. He never accepted money for his activities; he spied to free his country from Communism.

In the fall of 1981, Kuklinski knew he was close to being uncovered and asked the C.I.A. for help. He revealed the truth about his double life to his wife and two sons and all four of them were immediately taken out of Poland. In 1984, Colonel Kuklinski was sentenced to death *in absentia* by a Polish military court and his property was confiscated. In the 1990's, two of his sons lost their lives under unclear circumstances. The fall of communism in Poland brought about a debate whether Kuklinski was a hero or a traitor? It was not until 1998, that the sentence against him was dropped, and he was restored to the rank of a colonel, and was able to visit Poland.

Kuklinski died of a stroke in a military hospital in Tampa, Florida on February 11, 2004. He was buried with honors at Powazki Cemetery in Warsaw. In his obituary, the Director of the Central Intelligence Agency called him "a true hero of the Cold War to whom we all owe an everlasting debt of gratitude (…) It is in great measure due to bravery and sacrifice of Colonel Kuklinski that his own native Poland, and the other once-captive nations of Central and Eastern Europe and the former Soviet Union, are now free."

LIBERACE (1919-1987)
World's Highest Paid Musician

Wladziu Valentino Liberace was born in the suburbs of Milwaukee, Wisconsin as one of the four children of Frances Zuchowski (a Polish American) and Salvatore Liberace (an immigrant from Italy). From his early childhood Wladziu showed an unusual musical talent and was soon hailed a child prodigy. At the age of four he learned to play the piano by ear and already as a teenager he earned money playing popular tunes in movie theatres and speakeasies. At the same time Wladziu studied the technique of the world famous Polish pianist Ignacy Jan Paderewski, whom he met personally at the age of eight, after Maestro's concert in Milwaukee. When Paderewski became a friend of the Liberace family, he recommended the young artist for a scholarship at the Wisconsin Conservatory of Music. In 1939, after his classical concert, the audience wanted an encore. Liberace played a popular tune *Three Little Fishes* in a semi-classical style which the audience loved and which became the foundation of his later career. Soon he was performing in night clubs of many American cities on his custom-made piano with his candelabrum on top of it playing - as he called it himself - "classical music with the boring parts left out." At this time he took Paderewski's advice and adopted Liberace as his stage name, dropping both Wladziu and Valentino. In 1952 he began his television show, initially as a summertime replacement. After two years the show was carried by 217 American stations and was broadcast in 20 countries across the world. In 1953 Liberace attracted a capacity crowd at Carnegie Hall; soon afterwards he played for a record crowd of 16,000 at Madison Square Garden and for 110,000 people at the Soldier's Field Stadium in Chicago. Liberace became obscenely wealthy and he also spent lavishly, building dream houses with antiques and piano shaped pools, driving a Rolls Royce or a Bentley, wearing white mink furs and unusually big rings. He became more and more flamboyant, on and off stage.

Liberace also appeared in a few films, including the 1955 Warner Brothers production of *Sincerely Yours* where he appeared as the lead and played 31 songs. He also wrote a number of books from *Liberace Cooks*, which went into seven printings, to his best selling autobiographies.

In 1976 Liberace founded the non-profit Liberace Foundation for the Performing and Creative Arts which funds scholarships for schools and colleges across America. On April 15, 1979 The Liberace Museum was opened in Las Vegas where his legend lives on and serves as a major source of funds for the Foundation. Throughout the 1970's and the first half of the 1980's Liberace's live shows were major attractions in Las Vegas. His final performance was at Radio City Music Hall in November 1986. He passed away on February 4, 1987 at his home in Palm Springs due to AIDS and heart-related condition.

Among many awards that were bestowed on Liberace are two Emmy awards, six gold albums and two stars on the Hollywood Walk of Fame. *The Guinness Book of Records* lists Liberace as the world's highest paid musician and pianist.

BRONISLAW MALINOWSKI
(1884 - 1942)
Father of Social Anthropology

Generally considered to be one of the most important anthropologists of the twentieth century, the "Father of Social Anthropology," and the developer of "Functionalism," Malinowski was born in Krakow on April 7, 1884. His father was a university professor and his mother the daughter of a family with large landholdings. Perhaps through his father's influence, Malinowski stayed close to home to earn his doctorate at the celebrated Jagiellonian University in 1908. Developing an interest in anthropology during two years of further studies at the University of Leipzig, he traveled to England to study with well-known English anthropologists in London. As part of his study program, he went first to Papua, New Guinea, and then to the Trobriand Islands to conduct field research. Once there, Malinowski learned the Trobriand language, participated in their social life, and developed the process of "participant observation" that is the keystone for much of original research undertaken in modern anthropology and ethnography. His book, *Argonauts of the Western Pacific*, published in 1922, brought him unprecedented critical acclaim winning for him a reputation as one of the foremost anthropological scholars in the world. Malinowski taught in Great Britain in the post-war years, undertaking field work along with Radcliffe Brown in Africa in 1934 where the two documented African tribal life. Among his better-known studies during this time were *Crime and Custom in Savage Society* (1926) and *The Sexual Life of Savages in North-Western Melanesia* (1929).

During World War II, Malinowski settled permanently into a position at Yale University. At a time when "field research" was generally conducted through structured interviews, Malinowski is credited with introducing the methodology of "participant observation" as a research approach in which the researcher becomes a part of the community being studied so as to understand the complex social relationships through first-hand experience. He also challenged assumptions of the universality of Western views, pioneering a cross-cultural approach in *Sex and Repression in Savage Society* (1927). Malinowski argued that various cultures of the world must be understood within the view of the people who inhabit them, rather than those who look at them from afar. Much of what Westerners believed to be universal about human nature, he argued, was actually rooted in their own beliefs developed within a particular time and culture. His research also provided evidence that the linear view of societal development espoused by Social Darwinists was incorrect.

In 1942 he was among the six founders of Polish Institute of Arts and Sciences of America which was in fact Polish Academy of Arts and Sciences in exile.

CZESLAW MILOSZ (1911-2004)
Winner of the Nobel Prize for Literature

One of the major poets of the 20th c., prose writer, translator, professor of Slavic Languages and Literatures at the University of California in Berkeley; Nobel Prize winner for Literature in 1980. He was born on June 30, 1911 in Szetejnie, a small town in Lithuania, which, as a result of the earlier partitions of Poland was, at that time, part of the Russian Empire. His family settled in Vilnius in 1921 and this was where Milosz acquired secondary education, studied literature and law at the University of Stefan Batory from which he received an MA in law. His first volume of poetry was published in 1933. In 1936 he started working for Polish Radio, originally for Radio Vilnius and after being dismissed for being too liberal, for Warsaw Radio.

During World War II, the poet lived in Warsaw and was active as an underground writer. Towards the end of the war, in 1944, he married Janina Dluska. In 1946 Milosz joined the Polish diplomatic service and worked as the cultural attaché of Poland in Washington and in Paris. Disillusioned with the communist regime, he defected and sought political asylum in France in 1951. He started working closely with the Literary Institute headed by Jerzy Giedroyc. Soon the Institute published one of Milosz's most important books *The Captive Mind* (1953) in which he exposed the destruction of the intelligentsia by the communist regime.

In 1960 Milosz was offered professorship at the University of California at Berkeley, which he accepted and moved to the United States with his family. Ten years later he became a U.S. citizen. He wrote both poetry and prose as well as translated not only his own works into English but also Shakespeare, Milton, T.S. Eliot and others into Polish. He was one of the most popular lecturers on campus until his retirement from the University in 1978.

In the 1970s, *The Captive Mind* was translated into English and Milosz published a few collections of his poems in English. His literary work brought him recognition in the English-speaking world, followed by a number of prestigious literary awards including the Nobel Prize for Literature in 1980 for his lifetime achievements. This award made Milosz one of the best-read poets in the United States. The political thaw in Poland, which followed the birth of *Solidarity*, allowed Milosz to visit Poland in 1981, for the first time since his defection. He came in the glory of a national bard, the first Polish Nobel Prize winner for literature since Wladyslaw Reymont in 1924. His works were published in Poland for the first time in 30 years. A Nobel laureate, Milosz received numerous distinctions and honorary doctorates, including the National Medal of the Arts granted by the U.S. National Endowment for the Arts in 1989. He was also honored by Yad Vashem as one of "The Righteous among the Nations." In 1994 he received the Order of the White Eagle - the highest Polish decoration of merit.

After the collapse of communism in Poland in 1989 Milosz returned to his homeland and settled down in Krakow with his second wife Carol Thigpen, former dean at Emory University who after their marriage in 1992 became the poet's best agent and assistant. Milosz kept writing almost until his death in August of 2004. Following one of the most outstanding funeral ceremonies in the history of Krakow, the poet was buried at the crypt of the historic Skalka Church - the place reserved only for greatest of the greatest Poles.

EDMUND MUSKIE (1914 - 1996)
US Presidential Candidate

Edmund Muskie was a Democratic politician who served as Governor of Maine, U.S. Senator, Secretary of State and candidate for Vice President and President of the United States. Edmund Muskie's father Stephen Marciszewski was born in Poland in 1882. He left Poland as a teenager and immigrated to England first, but ultimately arrived in the United States in 1903. He changed his name to Muskie, married Josephine Czarnecka, and settled in Rumford, Maine. It was Edmund, their second child, who was born on March 28, 1914.

Edmund received his education at Bates College and Cornell University where he earned a degree in law in 1939. During World War II, he served in the Navy until being discharged in 1945. After the end of the war, Muskie returned to Maine and began practicing as a lawyer. He married Jane Gray. At that time he also started his political career, unexpectedly winning his bid to the state legislature. In 1954 he became the Governor of Maine. Soon he gained considerable popularity both among Democratic and Republican voters. In 1958 he was elected to the U.S. Senate as the first Democratic Senator from Maine in almost a century. He was reelected to this post in 1964, 1970 and 1976. He became known as a leading campaigner for stronger measures to cut down on pollution and to protect the natural environment which earned him the nickname of "Mr. Clean." He also earned a reputation as an expert in drafting and enacting legislation. Among many of his legislative successes was the 1973 War Powers Act which was passed over President Nixon's veto and which defined presidential and congressional powers in war-making decisions. Among other things, Muskie supported the vote for 18-year-olds, civil rights measures and federal aid for education. He served as Chairman of the U.S. Senate Budget Committee from 1973 until 1980.

In 1968 Muskie was nominated for Vice President of the USA. Running with the then sitting Vice President Hubert Humphrey they lost the election to the Nixon - Agnew team. In the 1972 presidential election, Muskie was considered a leading Democratic candidate for the Presidency. He announced his decision to run for the office in January but stayed in the race only until April when he withdrew. The reason for his withdrawal was certainly his defeats in the primaries in a few states, but he also became a victim of Nixon's "dirty tricks". Prior to the New Hampshire primary a letter was published in the Manchester Union-Leader which accused the Senator's wife of drinking and using off-color language during the campaign. Trying to defend his wife, Muskie made a very emotional speech. The press reported that he was crying. Even though he denied saying it was the snowflakes which melted on his face, this incident, as he admitted himself, "changed people's mind about what kind of a guy he was" and he soon was out of the race.

In 1980 Muskie became the Secretary of State in President Carter's Administration following the resignation of Cyrus Vance over the Iran Hostage Crisis. He tried to solve the crisis by diplomatic means and negotiated the release of the American hostages. Muskie retired from political life in 1981 after Jim Carter lost to President Reagan. He returned to Maine to practice law. He died of a heart attack on March 26, 1996 just two days shy of his 82nd birthday. He is buried at Arlington National Cemetery.

POLA NEGRI (1897 - 1987)
The Vamp of the Silent Cinema

A famous vamp of the silent cinema, and the first European actress to make a career in Hollywood. This stunningly beautiful woman popularized painted toenails and wearing turbans in America in the mid 1920's. She was the wife of a count and a prince, both of whom she divorced, and a mistress of Charlie Chaplin and Rudolf Valentino. She sued a French newspaper which printed reports of her romance with Hitler and won a 10,000 franc compensation.

Her real name was Barbara Apolonia Chalupiec. She was born in a small town in Poland on January 3, 1897. She was an only child in a poor family, brought up only by her mother after her father had been arrested by the Russians and sent to Siberia where he died in a labor camp. When she was five, they moved to Warsaw where Pola was admitted to the Imperial Ballet. Soon afterwards she was forced to give up her dancing career because of tuberculosis. She moved to the Imperial Academy of Dramatic Art and became an actress. Her stage debut came as early as 1913 and was followed the next year by her first film called *Slaves of Sin*.

In 1917, after making nine films in Poland, she went to Germany where she worked with Max Reinhardt and Ernst Lubitsch. Among the films she starred in was *Madame Dubarry*, released in America under the title of *Passion*, with which she earned a contract with Paramount Pictures. She came to Hollywood in 1922 and during the next few years made 20 films, all box office hits. *The Spanish Dancer*, *Forbidden Paradise*, *Hotel Imperial*, *Men*, and *Shadows of Paris* were among her best known titles. Pola Negri became the star of Hollywood, and her vamp roles made her very popular.

In 1926, during the funeral of Rudolph Valentino in New York, Pola publically collapsed. She took his body on a train across America stopping at a number of stations to let Valentino lovers pay tribute to him. However, the press accused her of trying to gain more publicity herself and her fans turned slowly away from her. This decline in popularity came together with the introduction of talkie movies which was a bad change for Pola. Her heavy accent that she could not get rid of and her rather harsh voice did not foretell her a brilliant career in sound pictures. Additionally, the Hays Office imposed a ban on scenes of passion and excessive kissing, which, in her case, proved rather disastrous.

A year later she was in Paris getting married to a Georgian prince who soon squandered most of her fortune. She returned to Hollywood in 1932 to make her first talkie *A Woman Commands*, but the reception of the film was lukewarm. Pola Negri returned to Germany where she continued to appear in films until the outbreak of World War II. She then moved to Paris and in 1941 returned to America. She made only two more films: *Hi Diddle Diddle* (1943) and Walt Disney's production *The Moonspinners* (1964). Pola Negri spent the rest of her life living quietly in California and then in Texas. In 1970 she published her autobiography entitled *Memoirs of the Star*. She died in San Antonio on August 1, 1987. Her star on the Walk of Fame in Hollywood is at 6933 Hollywood Boulevard. She was the 11th star in Hollywood history to place her palm and foot imprints in front of Grauman's Chinese Theatre.

JAN NOWAK JEZIORANSKI
(1919 - 2005)
Our Man in the White House

Journalist, writer, politician, "a great Polish freedom fighter and American patriot" as President George W. Bush called him on the day Jan Nowak died.

He was born in Berlin in 1919 as Zdzislaw Jezioranski and he adopted the name Jan Nowak as his *nom de querre* during World War II. After finishing his studies in 1936, he started working at Poznan University. When World War II broke out he was drafted into the army and fought in artillery. He was taken prisoner but managed to escape. After joining the Polish underground, he was assigned the role of a special envoy whose task was to force his way to London to report to the Polish Government in Exile and to the allies about the situation in occupied Poland. He made five daring trips as a courier between the Home Army and the Polish Government in Exile in London which earned him the name of the "Courier from Warsaw". After yet another of his missions, he returned to Warsaw shortly before the outbreak of the Warsaw Uprising on August 1, 1944. He took active part in the battle and a few days before capitulation he was ordered by the commander of the Home Army to go to London again. He managed to reach London as the first eyewitness of the uprising bringing with him a lot of documents and photographs.

After the war Nowak remained in London and worked for the Polish section of the BBC. In 1951 he moved to Munich in Germany and became head of the Polish Section of Radio Free Europe - a U.S. funded service in Polish which for millions of Poles was the primary source of information about what was really happening in their own country. Upon his retirement in 1976, Jan Nowak moved to Washington and became one of the leaders of the Polish community in America. He worked as National Director of the Polish American Congress and also served as an advisor to the American National Security Agency. After 1995 he was one of the key supporters of Poland's membership in NATO. His dream came true when Poland joined the organization in 1999. His remarkable feats of bravery during World War II, his dedicated service in Radio Free Europe and tireless advocacy of Polish interests in America earned him unprecedented respect among American politicians and Polish American leaders who all considered him the most influential Pole in Washington. All doors were open for him and he had an opinion of the man whom no one in Washington could refuse. Whether it was during the administration of Reagan, Bush Senior or Clinton, Jan Nowak always had a special pass which allowed him to park his car in a small street between the White House and the Old Exchange Building where all the most important government people worked. In 1996 he received the Presidential Medal of Freedom - the highest American civilian award for exceptionally meritorious service. In 2002, having fulfilled the mission of his life and happy to see "Poland (which) is now a normal country, free and secure, a member of NATO" Jan Nowak decided to return to Warsaw. He died in January of 2005.

IGNACY JAN PADEREWSKI
(1860- 1941)
Modern Immortal

Composer, pianist, philanthropist, statesman, Prime Minister of Poland - one of the greatest men in the history of Poland whom President Franklin Delano Roosevelt called a "modern immortal".

Paderewski was the greatest pianist of his time whose artistic career spanned over five decades from his first recital in the famous Salle Erard in Paris in 1888. He played for crowned heads, presidents and millions of people who truly loved this man. He composed two operas, a symphony, a violin and piano sonata, a number of songs and many piano pieces, including his best known minuet in G major. His American debut came on November 17, 1891 when he was the first artist to perform solo in the newly opened Carnegie Hall. In the next three months he toured America giving over 100 concerts and gaining unmatched popularity. It was followed by a number of American tours during which Paderewski traveled with five pianos in his own railway car. In 1902 his opera *Manru* had its American premiere at the Metropolitan Opera House.

In time Paderewski combined his artistic career with his political activities. After the outbreak of World War I he organized the General Committee for Aid to Polish Victims of the War. In April 1915 he arrived in the United States with a mission to help Poland. He issued many appeals to the Polish American Community for aid for Poland. While addressing a crowd of over 15,000 Poles gathered in Chicago in May 1915, he urged them to donate a day's work to Poland on July 15, the anniversary of the battle of Grunwald in 1410, one of the greatest military victories of the Polish army. In 1916 his concerts at the White House gave him an opportunity to meet President Woodrow Wilson a few times and to discuss the Polish topical issue of the day. Paderewski became an unquestionable leader of all Poles in America and was appointed a representative in the United States of the newly formed Polish National Committee. His activities brought about President Wilson's famous speech on New Poland in which he stated: "Take it for granted that statesmen everywhere are agreed that there should be a united, independent, autonomous Poland". This then turned into point 13 of Wilson's 14 point plan for the world, which ensured independent Poland after 123 years of partitions. Enthusiastically welcomed by the Polish people, Paderewski arrived in Warsaw on January 2, 1919.

The compromise between him and the Head of State Marshal Jozef Pilsudski resulted in Paderewski becoming Prime Minister and Minister of Foreign Affairs of independent Poland. In June he signed the Versailles Peace Treaty. In December of 1919 Paderewski resigned from the position of Prime Minister and became Poland's first delegate to the League of Nations. Shortly afterwards he retired from politics and resumed his artistic career.

In 1922 Paderewski returned to the USA and gave a concert in front of 16,000 people at Madison Square Garden. A year later, during his 13th tour of America, he gave another concert at Carnegie Hall, which was enthusiastically received by the audience and critics alike. In 1936 he performed in the film called *The Moonlight Sonata*.

In 1939 Poland was invaded by the Germans and the Soviets, World War II broke out and Paderewski, despite his old age and ill health, traveled to Paris to take up his political activities again. He became Head of the National Council in Exile. Upon invitation of President Roosevelt, he sailed to America with a view to undertaking measures in aid of the Polish cause. In June of 1941, after one of the rallies in New York, Paderewski fell ill. He passed away on June 29, 1941 at the Buckingham Hotel in the heart of Manhattan, almost opposite Carnegie Hall. His funeral at St. Patrick's Cathedral was attended by some 40,000 people. Afterwards his coffin was transported on a gun carriage to Pennsylvania Station and from there by a special train to Washington D.C. The coffin was laid in state at the Embassy of Poland where within one day over 5 thousand people filed past the casket. By a special decree of President Roosevelt, Paderewski was buried at Arlington Cemetery even though he was not an American citizen. The assumption was that he would remain there until Poland became free again. In 1992 a special committee organized the last journey of Paderewski to his home country. His remains were interred in the crypt of St. John's Church in Warsaw. His heart, however, stayed in America forever and is enclosed in an urn at the National Shrine of Our Lady of Czestochowa in Doylestwon, Pennsylvania.

Among special places in America closely connected with Paderewski is Rancho San Ignacio, near Paso Robles in northern California. Suffering from arthritis, the artist came there in 1913 for hot mud treatment and sulfuric water baths. Three months later he resumed his concert tour. He considered himself a resident of Paso Robles and returned there many times between 1914 and 1939. He is said to have introduced zinfandel grapes to the area which he planted on the rancho he purchased. The wines produced from these grapes won several awards and Paso Robles is now famous for the single varietal. The city of Paso Robles continues to organize an annual festival which celebrates the legacy of Ignacy Paderewski.

FRANK PIASECKI (1919-2008)
Vertical Flight Inventor

Vertical flight pioneer Frank Piasecki was born in Philadelphia on October 24, 1919 in a family of Polish immigrants. As a teenager he worked in local companies making autogiros. To further his education he studied mechanical engineering at Pennsylvania University and received a degree from Guggenheim School of Aeronautics of New York University. In 1940 with the help of his friends he founded a small aviation company which they called PV Engineering Forum. Three years later Piasecki built his first mono rotor helicopter PV-2. It was the second helicopter in America following the invention of Igor Sikorsky from 1939. Rumor has it that when Piasecki arrived in Washington to demonstrate his helicopter to military dignitaries, he was asked for a pilot license. It turned out he did not have one. He was granted a helicopter license instantly and became the first person to possess it without having the license for fixed-wing aircraft first. The PV-2 type was not put into series production and Piasecki started working on a twin-rotor helicopter. Piasecki's invention was that he placed the two rotors at different heights at each end of the helicopter's fuselage thus eliminating the collision of the air masses created by the rotors and making piloting easier. Besides, the helicopter with one rotor at each end could carry three times the weight of the conventional helicopter. The first tandem-rotor model, PV-3 Dogship, was flown on March 7, 1945. It was the biggest helicopter in the world at that time capable of carrying 10 people. It was called "the flying banana" because of the bend in its fuselage which ensured that the front and the back rotors did not collide. In May 1952 Piasecki's company introduced another model which was capable of carrying twenty people. In 1953 they designed the world's first twin-turbine helicopter, which could carry up to 40 passengers. In 1955, as a result of some dispute in the Board, Piasecki, together with some of his co-workers, left Piasecki Helicopter Corporation. His original company was renamed to Vertol and eventually sold to Boeing. For over 40 years the pride of Boeing Vertol (since 1987 called Boeing Helicopter Division) have been two helicopter's models *Sea Knight* and *Chinook*, which played a critical role in the Vietnam war and all major conflicts afterwards. The inventor's new company called "Piasecki Aircraft Corporation Pioneers in Vertical Flight" continued to work on advanced helicopter technology and its founder was actively working in it until his death in February 2008. Mr. Piasecki was awarded over 25 patents in the aerospace field.

In 1986 President Ronald Reagan awarded Frank Piasecki with the National Medal of Technology, the highest American technical honor. After the fall of the Berlin Wall President George Bush Sr. asked him to visit his native Poland and help rebuild Polish helicopter industry, which he gladly agreed to do.

Piasecki was married to Vivian O'Gara Weyerhaeuser. They had two daughters and five sons, two of whom are current vice presidents of the company.

EDWARD PISZEK (1916-2004)
Frozen Food Magnate

Polish American industrialist and philanthropist, co-founder of the Mrs. Paul's frozen fish concern.

He was born in Chicago in 1916 in a family of Polish immigrants who came to America at the beginning of the 20th century. Their family name was Piszczek - one of these Polish surnames virtually unpronounceable to most Americans. When he was in his twenties he legally shortened it to Piszek to ease the suffering of all the English speaking.

The family soon moved to Philadelphia where Edward's father opened a grocery. Edward graduated from Wharton School at the University of Pennsylvania, earning a degree in business administration. In these early days he worked for Campbell Soup Co. and then for General Electric. In 1946 the plant went on strike, but Edward needed money so he started selling food. Customers loved his crab cakes and business developed better and better. One day they made too many crab cakes and sold only little part of what they had prepared. Instead of throwing the rest into a garbage can, they threw it into a freezer at the back of the shop. A week later they tasted fine. It was the beginning of a frozen seafood empire. Having just $ 350 to invest, he and his friend John Paul set up a business - Mrs. Paul's Kitchens. In 1950 Piszek bought it from his partner and in 1982 he sold it to Campbell Soup Co for over $70 million.

Ed Piszek's philanthropy was equally enormous. Since the incident in 1964 when an Afro-American representing CARE organization walked into his office asking for a donation for an ambulance for the people of Tarnow, Poland, Piszek discovered his other goal - helping his native Poland. He shipped a fleet of mobile X-ray clinics, ambulances, support vehicles and lots of other equipment which contributed a great deal in Poland's fight against tuberculosis. He then founded the Copernicus Society, bought the Philadelphia House where Tadeusz Kosciuszko once lived, and donated it to the National Park Service. He spent hundreds of thousands dollars on a campaign to promote the culture of Poland and to change its image from that associated mainly with Polish jokes. His donations to the Little League Baseball in Poland made the Polish town of Kutno the European baseball training center. At the time when *Solidarity* was born in Gdansk and Poland suffered from severe food shortages Piszek donated ten million pounds of food to his homeland. In the 1980's he successfully persuaded his close friend James Michener to write his novel *Poland*, which soon became a bestseller.

Over the years he befriended two most important Poles: Karol Cardinal Wojtyla who later became Pope John Paul II and Lech Walesa - the legendary leader of the *Solidarity* movement. Piszek liked to call himself "the Polish Ben Franklin", because - as he admitted in one of his interviews - Franklin was the person he would like to be most. He even had his own copy of the Liberty Bell which was actually rung during the celebration of 200th anniversary of the United States in 1976.

Piszek died in March of 2004 at his house in Fort Washington outside Philadelphia, which was once George Washington's headquarters. He was 87. He devoted much of his long life to helping others.

Edward Piszek was undoubtedly an outstanding Polish American and if one has not heard about him so far it is only because of his unusual modesty.

ARTHUR RUBINSTEIN (1887-1982)
Piano Virtuoso who Could Play Before He Was Able to Speak

One of the greatest piano virtuosi of the 20th c. was born in Lodz, Poland on January 28, 1887 as the youngest of seven children of a Jewish family. His musical talent was evident at a very early age, and he learnt to play the piano earlier than he was able to speak. Rubinstein suffered from a syndrome of delayed speech and did not start speaking until he was about three. He made his first public appearance in his home town at the age of seven. He received his regular piano education in Warsaw under Aleksander Rozycki. He continued his education in Berlin under Joseph Joachim. At 12, Rubinstein made his debut in Berlin playing a Mozart piano concerto. At his Paris debut in 1904, he played, among other pieces, Chopin piano concerto No 2. Following the contract signed with the Knabe Piano Company, Rubinstein toured the United States in 1906.

He debuted at Carnegie Hall and even though his reception was rather cool, he continued with over 70 concerts visiting Chicago, Philadelphia and Boston.

In subsequent years he continued touring Europe and playing concerts in Vienna, Rome, and London. In 1932 he married Aniela Mlynarska, the daughter of a conductor Emil Mlynarski. The start of the family life made him return to working hard, practicing and performing. In 1937 he returned to Carnegie Hall, this time in his full artistic power. The outbreak of World War II and the looming German occupation of France forced him to move with his family to the United States. They settled in Los Angeles and Rubinstein became a U.S. citizen in 1946. He never again played in Germany in protest against Nazi crimes.

Rubinstein loved Poland and cared for it very much. He is especially remembered by Poles from the episode from the spring of 1945. He was playing at San Francisco Opera at the United Nations inaugural conference. When he noticed that among the flags displayed in the hall there was no Polish flag, he announced how outraged he was and played the Polish national anthem, which earned him a standing ovation of the audience. He returned to Poland a number of times to play concerts in Warsaw and in Krakow. In 1960 Rubinstein was honorary chairman of the jury of the 6th Chopin International Piano Competition which he himself opened by playing Chopin Piano Concerto in F-Minor with the Warsaw National Philharmonic Orchestra. He continued playing through his seventies and eighties, giving his last recital at Wigmore Hall in London in June of 1976. His piano career lasted over 80 years during which he performed more than 6 thousand times.

In 1977, at the age of 90 he left his wife for young Annabelle Whitestone. He died at the age of 95 in Geneva, Switzerland on December 20, 1982. In spite of his failing eyesight he managed to complete two volumes of his autobiography: *My Young Years* (1973) and *My Many Years* (1980). On the first anniversary of his death his ashes were buried in Jerusalem, Israel on a plot then named "Rubinstein Forest". In 1977 Rubinstein was made Honorary Knight of the British Empire. He received the French Legion of Honor, the Polish Officer's Cross of the Order of Merit, the American Medal of Freedom and a Grammy Lifetime Achievement Award in 1994.

MARCELLA SEMBRICH - KOCHANSKA (1858-1935)
First Lady of the Opera

One of the greatest sopranos in the history of the opera, the first Polish diva who made a career in the United States.

She was born as Prakseda Marcelina Kochanska on February 15, 1858 in a small village in Galicia. Her father, Kazimierz Kochanski, was a local music teacher. Later during her international career she adopted her mother's maiden name - Sembrich - as it was easier for Americans to pronounce. As a very young girl Marcella showed a great musical talent and she was taught to play both the violin and the piano by her father. She subsequently joined the Lvov conservatory where her teacher - Wilhelm Stengel - was only 12 years older than her and later became her husband.

To continue her education, she went to Vienna. This was where Franz Liszt discovered her vocal talent and encouraged her to develop her voice. Sembrich had her opera debut in 1877 in Athens. She continued her education and, at the same time, performed in Dresden and Milan. Finally, in 1880, she signed a contract with London's Covent Garden. She performed in a number of European countries before debuting in America in October of 1883. It was the premier season of the Metropolitan Opera and she sang the part of Lucia in *Lucia di Lammermoor*. At the benefit concert ending the 1883/1884 season she amazed the audience by playing a movement from a violin concerto, Chopin mazurka on the piano and singing a fragment of an opera by Giovanii Paisiello - all during the same evening. Despite the huge artistic success that the Met enjoyed during its first year, it was a terrible financial loss for the Opera. Kochanska was forced to return to Europe. She was back at the Metropolitan in 1898 and remained a resident soloist of this opera for ten seasons. She appeared in all most famous world operas. She also sang in Ignacy Paderewski's opera *Manru*, which was produced at the Met in 1902 and remains the only Polish opera staged there. Altogether she sang in over 450 performances earned a reputation of one of the greatest voices and the biggest star of the Met. She retired from the Metropolitan in 1909 at the height of her fame. At the end of her last season the company honored her with a special farewell gala. Sembrich continued to sing recitals until the death of her husband in 1917. After that she took to teaching first at the Julliard School of Music in New York, then at the Curtis Institute of Music in Philadelphia and finally at her own studio in Bolton Landing, NY. In 1937 *The Marcella Sembrich Opera Museum* was opened there with the mission of preserving the heritage of this great pianist, violinist, teacher, Polish patriot and benefactor.

Marcella Sembrich Kochanska died in New York on January 15, 1935. In its obituary, *The Washington Post* called her "the First Lady of the Opera". Pursuant to her last will she was buried in her husband's family vault in Dresden, Germany.

STANISLAW ULAM (1909-1984)
Key Mathematician of Manhattan Project

Stanislaw Ulam was born on April 13, 1909, at the beginning of a tumultuous historical period, in Lvov, a city that would be in the center of much of the coming turmoil. Growing to adulthood during the period of the Second Polish Republic, he took an early liking to mathematics, a subject in which professors at the Polytechnic Institute became famous as the "Lvov School" of mathematics. In 1938 he went to the United States on a fellowship at Harvard. Returning to Poland in the summer of the following year, he departed his homeland again on the eve of the German and Soviet invasion that began the Second World War. His remaining family in Poland perished in the Holocaust.

After gaining an appointment to the faculty of the University of Wisconsin, he was recruited by a friend, John von Neumann, to work on the Manhattan Project in Los Alamos, New Mexico. Among his subsequent contributions to America's nuclear research was his use of a modified Monte Carlo method for solving complicated mathematical problems dealing with chain reactions by using statistical sampling techniques. He is credited with providing an early mathematical proof that Edward Teller's design for a hydrogen bomb was flawed, and it was Ulam who solved the difficult problem of how to initiate a fusion reaction in a hydrogen bomb with his idea of using a fission bomb as the trigger for detonating the fusion device. Modified somewhat by Teller, it was Ulam's original idea that was eventually adopted as a process which is sometimes called the "Teller-Ulam Design."

Ulam is credited with refining Enrico Fermi's work on cosmic ray acceleration, developing the Fermi-Ulam Model or FUM, a computer prototype for studying non-linear dynamics and coupled mappings. He also invented the process of nuclear pulse propulsion, a method that is being evaluated for possible use in future spacecraft.

Ulam remained at Los Alamos until 1965 when he accepted the position of Chair of the Mathematics Department at the University of Colorado. His later work involved the application of mathematics to physics and biology. Among his contributions during this period was development of the technological singularity theory dealing with the acceleration of technological development and the changes that it brings to people.

MARIE ELIZABETH ZAKRZEWSKA (1829-1902)
Champion of Women's Rights

During the early nineteenth century there were no educational institutions in the United States in which women were regularly admitted to the study of medicine. One of the people whose efforts helped change this was Marie Elizabeth Zakrzewska. Born in Berlin in 1829 to a family that had to flee Poland because of its patriotic revolutionary activities, Zakrzewska became interested in medicine early on when she accompanied her mother in her work as a midwife at a local hospital. Frustrated with the lack of opportunity for women in the German society, she migrated to the United States in 1853 only to find few doors open to women interested in the medical profession. Her break came when she met Dr. Elizabeth Blackwell, one of only two or three female physicians in America, who managed to arrange for her admission to the Cleveland Medical College (later Western Reserve University).

Following graduation in 1856, Zakrzewska joined Blackwell in New York where they planned to open a hospital for women and children. Thanks in part to Zakrzewska's fundraising, the New York Infirmary for Women and Children, today known as Beth Israel Medical Center, opened in 1857. Two years later Zakrzewska moved to Boston where she was on the faculty of the New England Female Medical College until she opened the New England Hospital for Women and Children, now the Dimock Community Health Center in 1862. In addition to being only the second hospital in America to have an entirely female staff of physicians and surgeons the hospital also hosted as an intern Dr. Caroline Still, believed to be the first African-American female physician in America. In 1872 Zakrzewska opened as a new hospital program the first professional nursing program in the United States, which, among other "firsts", graduated the first African-American professional nurse in the country, Mary Elizabeth Mahoney. In addition to teaching, Dr. Zakrzewska had a strong private practice in gynecology. Dr. "Zak" was a familiar figure in her horse and buggy visiting patients around Boston. A year after her death, The New England Hospital for Women and Children published a memoir of her life.

A champion of women's rights and the abolitionist movement, Zakrzewska's pioneering work was largely responsible for the gradual opening of professional doors to women seeking to pursue careers in medicine.

KORCZAK ZIOLKOWSKI (1908-1982)

Designer and Sculptor of Crazy Horse Memorial

Over the years, Mount Rushmore has been a popular tourist destination as well as an inspiration for photographers, artists, and sculptors. One of the latter was Korczak Ziolkowski. Born in Boston in 1908, he was orphaned a year later, which may explain why he developed strong work ethics. After earning enough money to pay for his education at a local technical school, he became an apprentice at a Boston shipbuilding firm. Around 1918 he began to experiment with wood carving, gaining a reputation as a maker of fine furniture.

In 1932 he completed his first marble sculpture, a bust of Judge Frederick P. Cabot who had encouraged his boyhood interests in the fine arts. Quickly gaining a reputation throughout New England, he opened a successful studio in West Hartford, Connecticut, from which he produced a series of commissioned sculptures. In 1939 he received a major boost when his marble work "Paderewski, Study of an Immortal" was awarded the first prize at the New York World's Fair. In the same year he also began assisting Gutzon Borglum who was beginning his famous Mount Rushmore carvings of presidents George Washington, Thomas Jefferson, Abraham Lincoln, and Theodore Roosevelt.

Publicity from the World's Fair and his work on Mount Rushmore led Chief Henry Standing Bear of the Lakota tribe, whose heritage held the Black Hills of the Dakotas to be sacred land, to contact Ziolkowski with the suggestion that he create a memorial similar to Mount Rushmore as a tribute to America's Indian heritage. Intrigued by the idea, Ziolkowski met with representatives of the Lakotas, examined several potential sites, and began preliminary research for a massive sculpture that would be carved into a mountainside.

The outbreak of World War II interrupted planning for the monument when Ziolkowski volunteered for service in the U.S. Army. After landing on Omaha Beach during the landing at Normandy, he was wounded in action. Following his recovery and the end of the war, Ziolkowski moved to the Black Hills in 1947 to begin work on the "Crazy Horse Memorial," projected to be the largest sculpture in the world at 563 feet high and 641 feet wide. Sculpting commenced in 1948 with the dynamiting of the hillside to expose the rock and prepare the preliminary base for the final sculpture. For the next thirty-four years Ziolkowski worked on the immense project, refusing to take any salary for his efforts. However, work progressed slowly, since Ziolkowski also would not apply for grants or other funding, instead relying on admission fees paid by people interested in observing his work. Upon his death in 1982, his remains were buried at the foot of the mountain. His wife and several of his children have been carrying on his work.

ICONS OF TODAY

ZBIGNIEW BRZEZINSKI (b. 1928)
National Security Presidential Advisor

"Zbig", as he is often referred to by friends, currently serves as Counselor and Trustee at the Center for Strategic & International Studies and Robert E. Osgood Professor of American Foreign Policy at the Paul Nitze School of Advanced International Studies at Johns Hopkins University in Washington, D.C.

Zbigniew Brzezinski was born in Warsaw, Poland, in 1928. His father, Tadeusz Brzezinski, was a Polish diplomat who was posted to Germany, the Soviet Union, and finally to Canada. World War II and the results of the Yalta conference did not allow his family to return to Poland. In 1945 Brzezinski entered McGill University from which he obtained both his BA and MA degrees. He then went on to study at Harvard University where he received his PhD degree in 1953.

His activities in the U.S. Government included working as a member of the Policy Planning Council of the Department of State and as a National Security Adviser to Jimmy Carter, President of the United States, in the years 1977 -1981. He was awarded the Presidential Medal of Freedom in 1981 "for his role in the normalization of U.S.-Chinese relations and for his contributions to the human rights and national security policies of the United States." He later served as a member of the President's Chemical Warfare Commission, Member of the NSC-Defense Department Commission on Integrated Long-Term Strategy and Member of the President's Foreign Intelligence Advisory Board (a presidential commission to oversee U.S. intelligence activities).

From 1973 to 1976 he was Director of the Trilateral Commission. During the 1968 presidential campaign Brzezinski served as Chairman of the Humphrey Foreign Policy Task Force and in the 1976 presidential campaign as principal foreign policy adviser to Jimmy Carter. In 1988 he was Co-chairman of President Bush National Security Advisory Task Force. In addition to his political affiliations, Zbigniew Brzezinski was a member of the Boards of Directors of Amnesty International, Council on Foreign Relations, Atlantic Council, and the National Endowment for Democracy.

Zbigniew Brzezinski was on the faculty of Columbia University from 1960 to 1989 and on the faculty of Harvard University from 1953 to 1960. He is the author of numerous books on American politics and international relations. His latest bestseller is entitled *Second Chance*: *Three Presidents and the Crisis of American Superpower*.

Brzezinski serves as Honorary Chairman of AmeriCares, an international relief organization, and Co-Chairman of the American Committee for Peace in the Caucasus. He is a member of the Board of Trustees of the International Crisis Group and member of the Board of Directors of the Polish-American Enterprise Fund, Polish-American Freedom Foundation. He is a frequent public speaker, commentator on major domestic and foreign TV programs, and contributor to domestic and foreign newspapers and journals.

In the 2008 presidential campaign Zbigniew Brzezinski is considered to be the key foreign policy advisor to the Democratic candidate Senator Barak Obama.

JANUSZ GLOWACKI (b. 1938)
Author of Antigone in New York

Playwright, novelist, screenwriter, short story writer and essayist, Janusz Glowacki is the author of 9 plays, 11 books, 6 screenplays and 10 radio plays. Four of his movie scripts were produced in Poland, one directed by Oscar winning Andrzej Wajda. In 1999 his screenplay, *Hairdo*, won the Tony Cox Screenwriting Award in the Nantucket Film Festival Screenplay competition.

In August 1980, during the strike in the Gdansk shipyard, the cradle of *Solidarity* trade union movement, Glowacki spent time with the striking workers. He wrote the novel *Give Us This Day*, about the experience. The novel was stopped by censors and therefore published underground in 1981. Later the book was published in France, England, Germany, Switzerland, Turkey and Greece. In 1985, *Give Us This Day* was published by St. Martin's Mark in the U.S. However, Glowacki received most of his international recognition from his theatre plays. In December of 1981 he attended the opening of his play *Cinders* at the Royal Court Theatre in London. When martial law was declared in Poland in December 1981, he decided not to return to his country. He moved to New York in 1982 and has been living there since then. In 1984 *Cinders* was produced by Joseph Papp at the New York Shakespeare Festival, starring Christopher Walken and directed by John Madden. Glowacki's *Hunting Cockroaches*, a play about an émigré couple struggling to make it in New York, was originally produced at the Manhattan Theatre Club, (starring Dianne Wiest and Ron Silver, directed by Arthur Penn), followed by the Mark Taper Forum, (Swoosie Kurtz, Malcolm McDowell) and in more than 50 other professional theatres in the U.S. and world-wide. *Hunting Cockroaches* was cited by the American Theatre Critics Association as an Outstanding New Play in 1986. It received the Joseph Kesselring Award (1987) and the Hollywood Drama League Critics Award in 1987. *Time* magazine, as well as several other magazines, named the play *Hunting Cockroaches* as one of the ten best plays of the year.

Glowacki's play *Antigone in New York*, about three homeless people living in Manhattan's Tompkins Square Park, was originally produced at the Arena Stage in Washington D.C. It then had its New York premiere at the Vineyard Theatre, directed by Michael Mayer, and was translated into 20 languages and produced world-wide. In 1993 *Time* called it one of the best 10 plays of the year. Glowacki's most recent play, *The Fourth Sister* had its world premiere in January of 2000 in Warsaw. It was later produced in New York, Paris, Athens, Bratislava, Kiev, Budapest and Sofia, among others. His autobiographical novel, *Z glowy (Off the Top of My Head)*, published in 2004, was a number one bestseller for several weeks in Poland. Glowacki is also a recipient of the John S. Guggenheim Award and the National Endowment for the Arts.

RYSZARD HOROWITZ
(b. 1939)
Pioneer of Special Effects Photography

Ryszard Horowitz was born in Krakow, Poland on May 5, 1939. Four months later the Germans and Soviets invaded his homeland and his entire family ended up being sent to a series of concentration camps. They miraculously survived and at the end of the war were amongst the few Jewish families who were able to re-establish their lives in Krakow. Ryszard is one of the youngest known survivors of Auschwitz. In one of his interviews he said about his wartime experience: "Fortunately for me and part of my family we were under the wings of Oscar Schindler, and that's why I appear in Spielberg's movie which was based on the book by Tom McKinley called *Schindler*, which is the story of my family, my friends, and people very close to me". He became interested in photography when he was a small child. This was when he got his first simple and primitive camera. His first photo exhibition took place in his hometown when he was still in his teens. Ryszard studied art at the High School of Fine Arts in Krakow and then went on to major in painting at the Academy of Fine Arts there. In 1956, during a brief political and cultural thaw in Poland, the government awarded subsidies to encourage new and original art forms and Krakow suddenly emerged as a center of avant-garde jazz, painting, theater and filmmaking. Ryszard, who was seventeen at the time, took full advantage of being at the heart of the action and, consequently, became fascinated with American photography.

In 1959, he finally achieved his ambition of immigrating to the United States and enrolled at New York's famed Pratt Institute. While still a student at Pratt he received a scholarship to be apprenticed to Alexey Brodovitch, one of the most influential figures in the world of editorial design and photography at the time. After graduating from Pratt in 1963, Ryszard worked for a number of film and design companies and as an art director for Grey Advertising.

In November 1967 he left Grey and opened his own photography studio. Photography would be his lifelong career and passion. In the ensuing four decades his work has been exhibited, published and collected around the globe, and Ryszard has been awarded every major accolade that can be bestowed on a photographer.

He is recognized as a pioneer of special effects photography predating digital imaging.

JAN A.P. KACZMAREK (b. 1953)
Famous Composer and Oscar Winner

Jan A. P. Kaczmarek is a composer with a tremendous international reputation that continues to grow. He is a graduate of the Law Department at Adam Mickiewicz University in Poznan, Poland. Educated as a lawyer, he abandoned his planned career as a diplomat, for political reasons, to write music in order to finally gain freedom of expression. Initially, he composed for the highly politicized underground theater, and then for a mini-orchestra, *The Orchestra of the Eighth Day* which he created in 1977. The major turning point in his life, he says, was a period of intense studies with the avant-garde theater director, Jerzy Grotowski. He recorded his first album, *Music for the End*, in 1982 for Chicago-based Flying Fish Records. In 1989 he moved to Los Angeles. Jan's first success in the United States came in theater. After composing striking scores for productions at Chicago's Goodman Theatre and Los Angeles' Mark Taper Forum, Jan won an Obie and a Drama Desk Award for his music for the New York Shakespeare Festival's 1992 production of John Ford's *Tis Pity She's A Whore*. "Playing and composing was like a religion for me," Kaczmarek explains, "and then it became a profession." Having also composed music for films in Poland, he focused his attention to that medium, achieving recognition as a film composer with scores to such films as *Total Eclipse*, *Bliss*, *Washington Square*, *Aimée & Jaguar*, *The Third Miracle*, *Lost Souls*, *Edges of the Lord*, *Quo Vadis* and *Unfaithful*. In February 2005, Jan won an Oscar for Best Original Score in Marc Forster's highly acclaimed film, *Finding Neverland*.

J.A.P.K. also won The National Review Board's award for Best Score of the Year, and was nominated for both Golden Globe and the BAFTA's Anthony Asquith Award for Achievement in Film Music. In addition to his work in films, Jan was commissioned to write two symphonic and choral pieces for two important national occasions in Poland: *Cantata for Freedom* (2005) to celebrate the 25th anniversary of the *Solidarity* trade union movement and the oratorio *1956* (2006) to commemorate the 50th anniversary of the bloody uprising against the totalitarian government in Poznan, Poland. Both premieres were broadcast live on national television.

In 2007 Jan composed the score to the multi-national television series production of *War and Peace*. He also recorded the music to Janusz Kaminski's *Hania*, and the music to Thomas McCarthy's *The Visitor*. Jan is currently involved in setting up in Poland an Institute inspired by the Sundance Institute. It is anticipated that his *Rozbitek Institute* will begin accepting students in 2009.

JANUSZ KAMINSKI (b. 1959)
Steven Spielberg's Academy Award Cinematographer

Two-time Academy Award winner Janusz Kaminski was born in 1959 in Wroclaw, Poland, where he grew up with a passion for movies, the music of Pink Floyd and the freedom and well - being of the West. In 1980 he joined the amateur filmmaking club. While on holidays in Greece he met a defector from Poland who helped him go to the United States. Via Vienna, he came to New York and then to Chicago where he attended Columbia College from 1983 to 1987. Having moved to Los Angeles, he continued his education as a cinematography fellow at the American Film Institute Conservatory where he graduated with an M.F.A. degree.

As the director of photography in most of Steven Spielberg's films, Janusz Kaminski has created some of the most memorable images in the history of the cinema. Their famous cooperation started at the beginning of 1990s when he shot *Class of '61* at the director's invitation. Since then he has photographed all the best movies of Steven Spielberg starting with *Schindler's List* (1993) which brought him his first Academy Award and international acclaim (seven awards for best cinematography, including BAFTA - British Academy Award). It was followed by *Amistad* (1996) and *The Lost World: Jurassic Park* (1997). The second Academy Award for Kaminski was the result of his work on *Saving Private Ryan* (1998). Afterwards he worked with Spielberg on such films as *A.I.: Artificial Intelligence* (2001), *Minority Report* (2002), *Catch Me If You Can* (2002), *Terminal* (2004), *Munich* (2005) and the just released *Indiana Jones and the Kingdom of the Crystal Skull* (2008).

Janusz Kaminski's other film credits as a cinematographer include *Trouble Bound* (1992), *The Adventures of Huck Finn* (1993), *The Unbelievable Adventures of Pecos Bill* (1995), *How to Make an American Quilt* (1995), and *Jerry Maguire* (1996). In a very rare breakaway from Spielberg, Janusz Kaminski directed the photography in *The Diving Bell and the Butterfly* (2007), directed by Julian Schnabel, which brought him the fourth Academy Award nomination for Best Cinematography.

After a decade of his successes as a cinematographer, Kaminski made his directorial debut in the year 2000 with the thriller *Lost Souls*. His latest feature film *Hania* (2007) is the first film directed by Kaminski in Poland. The ravishing cinematography of *Hania* was provided by Kaminski himself while the music was composed by another Polish-born Oscar winner Jan A.P. Kaczmarek.

Today considered one of the best cinematographers in the history of cinema, Janusz Kaminski is a recipient of countless awards in many countries all over the world. He is a member of the prestigious American Society of Cinematographers (A.S.C.). In 2004 Kaminski married an ABC reporter Rebecca Rankin.

HILARY KOPROWSKI (b. 1916)
Discoverer of Polio Vaccine

A native of Poland, Hilary Koprowski, M.D. is a graduate of the Faculty of Medicine at Warsaw University. He also holds degrees from Warsaw Conservatory and Santa Cecilia Conservatory of Music in Rome.

Hilary Koprowski is the discoverer of the first vaccine against poliomyelitis, which was based on oral administration of attenuated poliovirus. His work on polio started in 1947 and the attenuated poliovirus was fed to the first child on February 27, 1950. During the ensuing ten years, the oral polio vaccine, developed originally by Hilary Koprowski, was used extensively for immunization against poliomyelitis on four continents. His vaccine was first used for mass immunization trials against poliomyelitis, which took place in Zaire (then the Belgian Congo) where 250,000 children were immunized orally within six weeks. At the same time, nine million children in Poland received the vaccine preventing paralytic poliomyelitis outbreaks. Today, the Western Hemisphere has been declared free of paralytic polio and the eradication of polio in the world is within sight. The pioneering work of Hilary Koprowski has made this possible.

Koprowski arrived at The Wistar Institute in Philadelphia in 1957 and served as its director for thirty-five years. Dr. Koprowski's longtime interest in rabies led to the development of a new type of vaccine for both humans and animals. He has also done pioneering work in the development of monoclonal antibodies, which are effectively used for the detection of cancer antigens and immunotherapy of cancer. In the years 1978-1980, Koprowski and his associates developed the first functional monoclonal antibody against colorectal cancer antigen and rabies.

In 1978, a new human rabies vaccine based on tissue culture was developed by Koprowski and the late Tad Wiktor. In the past decade, Koprowski directed his efforts towards the development of biomedical products in plants. He succeeded in producing a rabies vaccine in spinach and complete antibodies directed against rabies and cancer antigen in tobacco. Through cooperation with Polish scientists, it has been possible to conduct successful clinical trials with a Hepatitis B vaccine in lettuce.

Dr. Koprowski has received honorary degrees from numerous universities. He is a member of the National Academy of Sciences as well as the American Academy of Arts and Sciences and the New York Academy of Sciences. He is a Fellow of the College of Physicians of Philadelphia, which in 1959 presented him with its Alvarenga Prize. He serves as a consultant to the World Health Organization and the Pan American Health Organization. He holds foreign membership in the Yugoslav Academy of Arts and Sciences, the Polish Academy of Sciences, the Russian Academy of Medical Sciences, the Polish Institute of Arts and Sciences of America, and the Finnish Society of Sciences and Letters. Koprowski is the holder of the Order of the Lion of Finland, the French *Legion D'Honneur* Award, the Great Order of Merit presented to him by the President of Poland.

Dr. Koprowski is the author or co-author of over 890 articles in scientific publications and is co-editor of several journals. Currently, he is President of the Biotechnology Foundation Laboratories, Inc. and Head of the Center for Neurovirology at Thomas Jefferson University in Philadelphia.

MICHAEL KRZYZEWSKI (b. 1947)

Famous Coach K

Mike Krzyzewski's Polish grandfather Josef Pituch arrived in America from Austria by way of Ellis Island on March 21, 1906. He made his way to Waltersburg, Pennsylvania to work in the coal mines. After getting married and starting a family, the Pituchs eventually relocated to the Polish community in the inner city of Chicago. This was where their daughter Emily met her future husband, William Krzyzewski. The man who would come to be known as Coach K was born to Emily and William on February 13, 1947.

After attending the all-boys Catholic Weber High School in Chicago and developing his talents as a basketball player, Mike Krzyzewski was accepted by the United States Military Academy at West Point, where he played basketball under head coach Bobby Knight from 1967 to 1969. After graduating from West Point, Krzyzewski served five years as an officer in the United States Army.

Krzyzewski's college coaching career began as a graduate assistant to Bobby Knight at Indiana University from 1974 to 1975. Coach K's first head coaching position came just a year later at his alma mater where, for the next five years, he led the Cadets to a 73-59 record.

Appointed head coach of the Duke University Blue Devils Men's Basketball Team in 1980, Krzyzewski overcame some difficult early seasons to build one of the most successful collegiate athletic programs of all time. In his 28 years at Duke, Krzyzewski became the winningest coach in NCAA Tournament history. Krzyzewski's record offers evidence of his success: 730 total wins, 10 Final Four berths in the last 20 years, including five straight appearances from 1988 till 1992, 11 regular season ACC crowns and 10 Atlantic Coast Conference Tournament titles. But most impressive are the three national championships (1991, 1992 and 2001) that make Coach K one of only four coaches in NCAA history to earn three or more NCAA titles. Coach K owns a 803-267 career record while attaining a 730-208 mark at Duke. On March 1, 2008, Krzyzewski became the sixth coach in Division I history to reach 800 wins.

Such accomplishments have not gone unnoticed. In all, Coach K has been named the National Coach of the Year 12 times in eight different seasons. Coach K was presented by his college coach Bob Knight as one of three members of the Naismith Memorial Basketball Hall of Fame following the 2001 season. Krzyzewski added to his already impressive list of accomplishments on Sept. 26, 2005 when he was named head coach of the USA Basketball Men's Senior National Team program for 2006-2008. In the summer of 2007, he guided the USA squad to a gold medal victory and an unblemished 10-0 record in the FIBA Americas Championship. It automatically qualified team USA for the 2008 Olympics in Beijing, China where they won the gold medal.

In 1992, *The Sporting News* named him the Sportsman of the Year, becoming the first college coach to win the honor. The magazine said, "On the court and off, Krzyzewski is a family man first, a teacher second, a basketball coach third, and a winner at all three. He is what's right about sports…"

CARDINAL ADAM MAIDA
(b. 1930)
Archbishop of Detroit

Adam Joseph Maida was born on March 18, 1930, in East Vandergrift, Pennsylvania. He was the first of three sons born to Adam Maida and Sophie Cieslak Maida. Cardinal Maida's father came to the United States from a village near Warsaw, Poland. His mother was born in the United States and resided in Scott Township, Pennsylvania.

Cardinal Maida graduated from St. Mary's Preparatory, Orchard Lake, Michigan, in 1948. Following his graduation, He entered St. Mary's College in Orchard Lake, Michigan. In 1950, he transferred to St. Vincent's College in Latrobe, Pennsylvania, where he graduated in 1952 with a Bachelor of Arts degree in Philosophy. In 1956, Cardinal Maida graduated with a Licentiate in Sacred Theology (S.T.L.) from St. Mary's University in Baltimore, Maryland.

In 1960, Cardinal Maida received a Licentiate in Canon Law (J.C.L.) from the Pontifical Lateran University in Rome. In 1964, he was awarded a Doctorate in Civil Law (J.D.) from Duquesne Law School in Pittsburgh. Cardinal Maida was admitted to practice law before the Bar for the State of Pennsylvania, the Federal Bar in Western Pennsylvania, and the United States Supreme Court. On May 26, 1956 Cardinal Maida was ordained a priest in St. Paul Cathedral, Pittsburgh, by the then Bishop John Dearden. Following his ordination, Cardinal Maida served in the Diocese of Pittsburgh as associate pastor, Vice Chancellor and General Counsel of the Diocese, in the Diocesan Tribunal, and as Assistant Professor of Theology at La Roche College, and Adjunct Professor of Law at Duquesne University Law School.

On January 25, 1984 he was ordained and installed as the ninth Bishop of the Diocese of Green Bay, Wisconsin. On May 7, 1990 Pope John Paul II named Bishop Maida Archbishop of Detroit. He was installed as Archbishop of Detroit on June 12, 1990. On October 30, 1994 Pope John Paul II named Archbishop Maida Cardinal. He was elevated to the College of Cardinals at a Consistory held on November 26, 1994, at the Paul VI Auditorium in the Vatican. Being one of the most essential people in the American Catholic Church, Cardinal Maida works on a number of committees of the United States Conference of Catholic Bishops. He also serves as a member or consultant of a number of bodies of Roman Curia.

Cardinal Maida is currently on the Boards of Trustees of a number of Catholic organizations and institutions in the United States including: the Basilica of the National Shrine of the Immaculate Conception in Washington, D.C., the Catholic University of America in Washington, D.C., the Michigan Catholic Conference in Lansing, Michigan, the Papal Foundation in Philadelphia, Pennsylvania, the Ave Maria School of Law in Ann Arbor, Michigan, the SS. Cyril and Methodius Seminary in Orchard Lake, Michigan, the Sacred Heart Major Seminary in Detroit, Michigan and others. He is also President of the Pope John Paul II Cultural Center in Washington D.C. and President of Pope John Paul II Cultural Foundation in the United States.

LECH MAJEWSKI (b. 1953)
Artist, Filmmaker, Poet, Stage Director

Polish-American film and theatre director, writer, poet, and painter Lech Majewski was born In Katowice, Poland.

He studied at the Academy of Fine Arts in Warsaw and then at the National Film School in Lodz, Poland where he graduated in 1977. In the early eighties, after completing his film *The Knight* and in view of the declaration of the martial law in Poland, Majewski immigrated to England and then to the United States, where he has lived since 1981.

Working in the U.S., Brazil, England, Poland, Germany, Lithuania, France and Italy, Majewski builds his visions in his paintings, films, installations, novels, theater and opera stagings. His credits include such films as: *The Knight*, *Prisoner of Rio*, *Gospel According to Harry*, *Basquiat*, *Wojaczek*, *Angelus*, *The Garden of the Earthly Delights* and *Glass Lips*.

In 2006 The Museum of Modern Art in New York honored Mr. Majewski with a major retrospective of his works, entitled *Lech Majewski: Conjuring the Moving Image*. Curated by Laurence Kardish, the retrospective presented Majewski's films and video features. The world premiere of *Blood of a Poet*, a unique sequel of thirty-three video art pieces was the highlight of the opening night at MoMA. Exhibited later by many galleries and museums, *Blood of a Poet* was installed at the Berlinale in February 2007; and in June became a part of the 52nd Venice Biennale, where, for almost six months, it was shown in two locations: as the non-stop projection on Campo San Pantalon, and on multiple screens inside the Giudecca's Teatro Junghans.

The *Blood of a Poet* cycle was assembled into a single feature film entitled *Glass Lips*, which premiered at the Pacific Cinematheque in Vancouver. In November 2007, when the film opened in the U.S.A., a *New York Post* critic called it "one of the most unusual, beautiful films of the year."

In 2007, Lech Majewski Retrospective that originated at MoMA, traveled to The Art Institute of Chicago, the Portland Art Museum, the Cleveland's Wexner Arts Center, Seattle International Film Festival, the UCLA Film Archive, the Berkeley Art Museum, and The National Gallery in Washington D.C. Majewski is a member of the Directors Guild of America and the European Film Academy. His works have won many prestigious awards. His latest production of Karol Szymanowski's double bill - ballet *Harnasie* and opera *King Roger* - at at Bard College, in Annandale-on-Hudson, New York was received rather chilly by the critics but appreciated a lot by the opera lovers.

ADAM MAKOWICZ (b. 1940)
Master of Jazz Improvisation

Jazz legend, master of improvisation, piano virtuoso, voted Europe's Number One Jazz Pianist six years in a row by the readers of Polish jazz magazine *Jazz Forum*, decorated with the Officer's Cross of Merit of the Republic of Poland, he has recorded 37 albums and performed in the world's best concert venues, playing with the world's best musicians. He has composed music for string quartets and jazz trios, several piano pieces, over 100 short jazz compositions, as well as two movie scores.

At the age of 15 Makowicz became fascinated with jazz. In communist Poland jazz was a forbidden fruit, a product of the decadent West. That music, which Makowicz himself called "the world of freedom and improvisation", fascinated him to such an extent that upon attaining majority, he abandoned his school and family and chose his own way, basically living on the street for two years. Krakow-based jazz club *Helicon* became his oasis.

In 1977, on the recommendation of Benny Goodman and jazz promoter Willis Conover (whose radio program titled *Music USA-Jazz Hour* first exposed the young Makowicz to jazz music performed by the greatest stars from across the ocean), legendary producer John Hammond invited Makowicz to a 10-week tour of the U.S. During that trip Makowicz recorded his first solo album, *Adam* (CBS Columbia).

In 1978 he returned to America, this time on a six-month contract, which was subsequently extended. Manhattan became his home. All the legendary music venues opened their doors to him, including New York's Carnegie Hall (his first solo performance there was part of a concert dedicated to the memory of Erroll Garner, who had died six months before) and the Greenwich Village Cookery Club. He was also invited to the Newport Jazz Festival in Rhode Island. In the United States he has played with the greatest musicians such as Benny Goodman, Herbie Hancock, Earl Hines, Freddie Hubbard, Sarah Vaughan, Teddy Wilson, and George Shearing. Adam Makowicz has recorded over 30 albums so far.

He performs solo as well as with orchestras, such as the National Symphony of Washington, the London Royal Philharmonic Orchestra, the Moscow Symphony Orchestra, the Warsaw Philharmonic, the Chester String Quartet, and the Amici String Quartet. Makowicz also plays with percussion sections (George Mraz, Al Foster, Jack DeJohnette, Charlie Haden) and with string quartets. Recently he moved to Toronto, Canada where he continues his artistic career.

DANUTA MOSTWIN
(b. 1921)
Author of America! America!

With critical acclaim in the United States, Poland, England, France and other countries, Danuta Mostwin has been cited as the opener of a new chapter in Polish-American literature. Hailed as a writer who stresses themes of uprootedness and the resulting anxieties of the loss of identity, she had remarkable success with her own separate areas of identity. Danuta Mostwin experienced the pangs of post-World War II uprootedness from "political exile" through "refugee", "émigré-immigrant" to "displaced person" with all their xenophobic implications. In her scholarly writing on *The Transplanted Family* for her doctorate in Social Science at Columbia University and her fictional writing that includes stories, plays and fourteen novels, Mostwin deals with the anguish of the loss of identity plus the social, economic, political and psychological anxieties that confront individuals and families oppressed by uprootedness.

Born Danuta Pietruszewska in Lublin in August, 1921, she came from an educated, patriotic family with strong roots in Polish culture.

Danuta's biographical odyssey is as fascinating as her highly acclaimed novels that often reflect her life's adventures and displacement from Poland - from the time of her birth to her days in Warsaw during World War II, her subsequent escape with her husband and mother in 1944, through Czechoslovakia, Germany and Benelux, reaching London as an exile for several years. Then they departed for New York, finally arriving in Baltimore in 1951, where they continue to reside. Her journey was touched with terror, mystery, historical significance, economic deprivation, courage and total uprooting.

Professor Mostwin's publications began with *House of the Old Lady* which was followed by the highly acclaimed *America! America!*. Outstanding prizes and publications in Poland, England, France and other countries resulted in her collected writings (20 volumes) being chosen for publication in Torun, Poland in 2004. At the same time, the Ohio University Press, Polish and Polish-American Studies Series, began translating and publishing some of her work in English. With the publication of her dissertation, *The Transplanted Family*, Professor Mostwin introduced her original theory of "the third value," a unique interpretation of the two different cultural patterns which immigrants had to cope with.

Danuta Mostwin studied cultural anthropology and sociology at Columbia University under the supervision of Margaret Mead. Mostwin dedicated her research to the plight of the transplanted "displaced persons", forced to emigrate from their homeland and seeking their identity in a strange new land with different language, culture and mores. She began writing of alienation, embarking on social casework and developing her "third value" theory. She went on to study Social Work at the Catholic University of America in Washington, DC.

Danuta Mostwin's contribution to Polish-American literature is broad and profound. Her reach extend to literature-at-large. Because of the breadth of her oeuvre, the originality of her ideas, and her identity and empathy with her characters, she has been nominated twice, in 2006 and 2007, for the Nobel Prize for Literature.

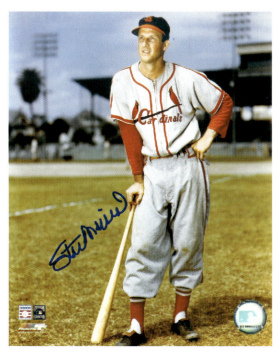

STANLEY MUSIAL (b. 1920)
"Stan the Man"

With 24 All-Star games, three MVP Awards, 475 homers, 331 batting average, 3630 hits, 1949 runs scored, three World Series rings, 1951 RBIs, 3026 games, seven batting titles, and a plaque in Cooperstown - Stanley Frank Musial (nicknamed "Stan the Man" and "the Donora Greyhound") is one of the most famous baseball players in the history of Major League Baseball.

He was born on November 21st, 1920 in Donora, Pennsylvania as the first son of Lukasz and Mary. His father was a Polish immigrant who was born and raised on a farm near Warsaw and came to America around 1909. Stanley grew up in the industrial area of Donora where his father was employed by the American Steel and Wire Company. On his 19th birthday Stan married Lillian Labash. They had four children: a son and three daughters. Musial started his career as a pitcher but a shoulder injury made him move to the outfield in 1940. Here is a short summary of his incredible 22-year-long career with the St. Louis Cardinals:

- Stan Musial was selected *the Sporting News* Major League Player of the Year in 1946 and 1951. *Sports Illustrated* named him its Sportsman of the Year in 1957 and *the Sporting News* honored him as Sportsman of the Decade for the years between 1946 and 1956.
- St. Louis Cardinals 1941 - 1963. 3,026 Games played. At bat 10,972 times. Scored 1,949 runs. 1,951 runs batted in. Total bases of 6,134. Led the National League in total bases and slugging percentage 6 years. Won 7 National League batting titles. Most Valuable Player 1943, 1946, and 1948. Named on 24 All-Star teams.
- Upon retirement, Musial held 17 Major League, 29 National League and 9 All-Star Game records. He was elected to The Baseball Hall of Fame in 1969.
- In 1954, Stan Musial became the first player to hit 5 home runs in a double header against the New York Giants.
- A statue of Musial was dedicated at Busch Stadium in St. Louis, MO in 1968.
- Musial played all of his 22 years of professional baseball with the St. Louis Cardinals.
- He was the first player in the national League who made 100,000 USD.

Following his retirement from baseball, Musial became a successful businessman and restaurateur. He remains a popular figure in St. Louis. In May of 2008 Stan was honored with the "Stan the Man" Day at Busch Stadium in St. Louis and part of Eighth Street in front of Bush Stadium was officially renamed "Stan Musial Drive".

RAFAL OLBINSKI (b. 1945)
Master of the Poster

Graphic artist, stage designer and surrealist painter - Rafal Olbinski immigrated to the United States in 1981, where he soon established himself as a prominent painter, illustrator, and designer. For his artistic achievements he received more than 150 awards including Gold and Silver Medals from the Art Directors Club of New York, Gold and Silver Medals from the Society of Illustrators in New York and Los Angeles, and The Big Crit 2000 Award by Critique Magazine in San Francisco. In 1994 he was awarded the International Oscar for The World's Most Memorable Poster, Prix Savignac in Paris.

In the same year he received the Creative Review Award for the best of British illustration in London. In 1995 his poster was chosen as the official New York City Capital of the World Poster, in an invitational competition by a jury headed by Mayor Rudolf Giuliani. In the following year he won the Stevan Dohanos Award for the best painting in the Annual Member Exhibition of the Society of Illustrators. In July 2002 the City of Fondi, Italy awarded him Premio Divina Guilia for his contribution to contemporary art. Rafal Olbinski's paintings are included in the collections of the National Arts Club in New York, the Smithsonian Institute and the Library of Congress in Washington, Suntory Museum in Osaka, Japan, and throughout Europe.

In 1996, he was commissioned by the U.S. Information Agency to design a poster celebrating the 25th Earth Day Anniversary. In 2002, a selection of Olbinski's paintings was included in the Great Art, Grand Space projection in Grand Central Terminal, as a highlight of the Earth Day Celebration in New York. The other artists presented in the show were Keith Haring, Roy Lichtenstein, Robert Rauschenberg, and Andy Warhol. In the same year his set design debut for the Opera Company of Philadelphia's performance of Mozart's Don Giovanni, was highly acclaimed by critics in *the New York Times* and *the Philadelphia Inquirer*.

Rafal Olbinski's work was featured in many articles by international magazines and newspapers including *The New York Times*, *Newsweek*, *Time*, *Business Week*, *Atlantic Monthly*, *Playboy*, *Omni*, *New Yorker* and *Der Spiegel*.

Five hard cover books on his art were published in the USA with the most recent *Olbinski's women* by Hudson Hills Press in 2007.

Rafal Olbinski is the author of the poster which appears on the cover of the present album.

SCOTT E. PARAZYNSKI (b. 1961)
Our Man in Space

This NASA astronaut was born on July 28, 1961, in Little Rock, Arkansas. Both his parental grandparents were of direct Polish descent and came to America through Ellis Island at the turn of the last century settling in upstate New York. Parazynski is married to the former Gail Marie Vozzella. They have two children. He enjoys mountaineering, rock climbing, flying, scuba diving, skiing, travel, woodworking, and nature photography. A commercial, multi-engine, seaplane and instrument-rated pilot, Dr. Parazynski has logged over 2000 flight hours in a variety of aircraft. As a mountaineer, his summits include Cerro Aconcagua (at 22,841 feet above sea level, the tallest mountain in the world outside of Asia) and 53 of Colorado's peaks over 14,000 feet in altitude.

Parazynski received a Bachelor of Science degree in biology from Stanford University in 1983, continuing on to graduate with honors from Stanford Medical School in 1989. He served his medical internship at the Brigham and Women's Hospital of Harvard Medical School (1990). He had completed 22 months of a residency program in emergency medicine in Denver, Colorado when selected to the Astronaut Corps.

While in medical school, he competed on the United States Development Luge Team and was ranked among the top 10 competitors in the nation during the 1988 Olympic Trials. He also served as an Olympic Team Coach for the Philippines during the 1988 Olympic Winter Games in Calgary, Canada.

NASA EXPERIENCE: Selected as an astronaut in March 1992, Dr. Parazynski reported to the Johnson Space Center in August 1992. He completed one year of training and evaluation, and was qualified as a mission specialist. He has served as the Astronaut Office Operations Planning Branch crew representative for Space Shuttle, Space Station and Soyuz training, as Deputy (Operations and Training) of the Astronaut Office ISS Branch, and as Chief of the Astronaut Office EVA Branch. In the aftermath of the Columbia tragedy, he was the Astronaut Office Lead for Space Shuttle Thermal Protection System Inspection and Repair.

SPACE FLIGHT EXPERIENCE: Scott Parazynski took part in 5 space flights: STS-66 - Space Shuttle Atlantis (1994); STS-86 - Space Shuttle Atlantis (1997); STS-95 - Space Shuttle Discovery (1998); STS-100 - Space Shuttle Endeavour (2001); STS-120 - Space Shuttle Discovery (2007). Altogether Parazynski logged over 1,381 hours (over 8 weeks) in space, including over 47 hours of ExtraVehicular Activity (EVA) during his seven space walks, and he travelled more than 23 million miles.

In May 2008 Scott attempted to climb Mount Everest. He was already within 24 hours of the summit when he had to come back due to severe back injury. He hopes to return and complete this mission one day.

ROMAN POLANSKI (b.1933)
Godfather of Modern Cinema

Film director, actor, writer and producer Roman Polanski was born in Paris but raised and educated in Poland. During World War II he spent two years at the Krakow Ghetto but then managed to escape and survived the war in the Polish countryside, living with different Catholic families. After the war he attended Art School in Krakow and then the Film Academy in Lodz which he completed in 1959. Being still a student Polanski made a few short films, including *Two Men and a Wardrobe* or *When Angels Fall,* which achieved critics' acclaim. In 1962 he made his first feature film *Knife in the Water* - a dark psychological thriller. Contrary to how it was received in Poland, *Knife in the Water* was a major commercial success in the West and earned Polanski international fame. It was nominated for an Academy Award as Best Foreign Language Film and was featured on the cover of *Time* magazine. Polanski's next films: *Repulsion* (1965), *Cul-de-sac* (1966) and *The Fearless Vampire Killers* (1967) were made in England. It was during the production of *The Fearless Vampire Killers* that he met a rising star Sharon Tate. The two got married in January 1968 and soon afterwards Polanski came to the United States. He established his reputation in Hollywood by making the psychological thriller *Rosemary's Baby* (1968). A year later Sharon Tate (and four other people) was brutally murdered by the infamous Manson gang at the couple's rented house in Hollywood Hills. Polanski left America for France. In 1971 he made his violent film version of Shakespeare's *Macbeth*. The director returned to Hollywood to make *Chinatown* (1974) for Paramount Pictures. The film was a great success and received an Oscar for Best Original Screenplay and 11 nominations for Academy Awards, including Best Picture and Best Director. *Chinatown* became Polanski's greatest commercial success and until today it has the reputation of a classic of New Hollywood cinema. Not before long, Polanski was accused of seducing a minor and had to flee from America to avoid prison. He has not returned to the United States since that time making all his later films in Europe. In 1979 he made *Tess* for which he received another Academy Award nomination as Best Director. The film won Oscars for Cinematography, Art Direction and Costume Design.

Polanski's most important films of the 80's include *Pirates* (1986) and *Frantic* (1988). Roman Polanski married a French actress Emmanuelle Seigner in 1989. He directed her in *Frantic*, opposite Harrison Ford and later in his films of the 90's: *Bitter Moon* (1992) and *The Ninth Gate* (1999).

In 2002 Polanski made *The Pianist* which is an adaptation of the autobiography of the same name by Jewish-Polish musician Wladyslaw Szpilman. This Holocaust story had deep connections with Polanski's own life at the time of the Krakow Ghetto. The film brought for Polanski an Oscar for the Best Director. A few months after the Oscar ceremony, Harrison Ford flew to France to present the award to Polanski. In 2005 the director shot *Oliver Twist* - a new adaptation of Charles Dickens's novel.

Polanski has directed many plays on stage. He also continues his acting career started in Poland at the age of 14. In 2002, he played one of the leading roles in Andrzej Wajda's film *Zemsta (The Vengence)*. In 2007 he appeared in Brett Ratner's *Rush Hour 3* and in 2008 in Antonio Luigi Grimaldi's film *Caos Calmo*. During the 2008 Sundance Film Festival a documentary *Roman Polanski: Wanted and Desired* premiered, which returns in details to the incident from 1978 and describes the strange manner in which the case proceeded. Polanski declined to participate in this movie.

STEFANIE POWERS (b. 1942)
Movie Star and Wildlife Preservation Activist

She was born as Stefania Federkiewicz to Polish American parents. Her ancestors on both her mother's and her father's sides came to America at the turn of the last century or just thereafter. Even though her mother or grandmother never spoke much about family background (their reluctance to do so was always excused by the assumption that things were very difficult for them) Stefanie learned quite a lot about it thanks to her San Francisco friend, Wanda Lubomirska, who helped her greatly to make a connection to Poland and to the pride she now feels by being Polish.

She began her career at the age of 15, dancing briefly for Jerome Robbins before her first movie role. Under a five-year contract with Columbia Pictures, she appeared in 15 motion pictures before her first television series, *The Girl from U.N.C.L.E.*. While under contract, she opened the San Francisco production *of Under the Yum Yum Tree*. Ten motion pictures followed, plus dozens of TV guest appearances, over 20 mini-series and tours in plays such as *How the Other Half Loves*, *Sabrina*, *A View from the Bridge*, and musicals such as *Oliver* and *Annie Get Your Gun*. Further television work brought two more television series, *Feather & Father Gang* and the long-running *Hart to Hart*. Stefanie toured extensively with Robert Wagner in *Love Letters*, including the play's London West End premiere. She returned to the West End in 1991 in the musical *Matador*. After completing eight two-hour television movie versions of *Hart to Hart*, she returned to the musical theatre in the first revival of *Applause*, the musical version of *All about Eve*. Furthering her involvement in Britain, Stefanie launched the premiere of a new American play, *The Adjustment*. After a short off Broadway run in *The Vagina Monologues*, she returned to England to star in the West End production of *The King and I,* which later toured the USA for ten months. Following *The King and I* tours a jazz CD was released on which Stefanie collaborated with veteran jazz musician/arranger Page Cavanaugh. Most recently *One from the Heart*, a one woman show of song and dance, was launched and will tour in 2009.

As much a part of her personal life as her professional career is her devotion to animal preservation and protection, which often seems more of a vocation than an avocation. As president of the William Holden Wildlife Foundation, she resides part time in Kenya overseeing the many projects ongoing in East Africa, she serves on the advisory board of three major zoos, is a fellow of the Los Angeles Zoo, the conservation consultant to Jaguar Motor Company and created the Jaguar Conservation Trust - a ground breaking corporate effort to preserve the animal the car uses as its name and symbol. And lastly, she has recently joined the advisory board of the Vanishing Herds Foundation's battle for the preservation of the last remnant of Asiatic lions, located in Gujarat, India.

EDWARD L. ROWNY (b. 1917)
Adviser to Five American Presidents

Edward L. Rowny was born in Baltimore, Maryland on April 3, 1917 in a family of Polish immigrants. His father immigrated to the United States from a small village near Warsaw in 1912. His mother's parents were from Poland, too.

Ed Rowny graduated from Johns Hopkins University in 1937 and the U.S. Military Academy in 1941. Rowny earned two Masters Degrees from Yale University (Engineering and International Relations) as well as a Doctor of Philosophy degree from American University.

During World War II he served in Liberia and fought in Italy. In the Korean conflict, he was a planner of the Inchon invasion and the official spokesman for General Douglas MacArthur. Rowny commanded the 38th Infantry Regiment and fought in seven Korean campaigns. In 1963 he headed the Army Concept Team in Vietnam (ACTIV), testing new concepts for counterinsurgency operations. From 1965 to 1969, Rowny commanded the 24th Infantry Division, planned and executed the withdrawal of U.S. troops and supplies from France (FRELOC) and served as Deputy Chief of Staff of U.S. European Command in Stuttgart, Germany. Rowny commanded I Corps in Korea in 1970-71. In 1971 he became Deputy Chairman of the NATO Military Committee and initiated the Mutual and Balanced Force Reduction (MBFR) negotiations.

From 1973 to 1979 Rowny was the Joint Chiefs of Staff Representative to the Strategic Arms Limitation Talks (SALT II) in Geneva. He served longer than any other U.S. delegate - 6 ½ years - and negotiated for more than 1,000 hours. General Rowny retired from the Army in 1979. From 1981 to 1984, Rowny served as a chief negotiator in Strategic Arms Reduction Talks (START) in the rank of an ambassador. As the head of START, he negotiated an additional 1,000 hours. From 1985 until 1990, he was a Special Advisor for Arms Control to Presidents Reagan and Bush.

In June 1990, Rowny retired from the government to become a consultant on international negotiations. During Reagan's second term he served as Special Advisor to the President for Arms Control.

President Reagan awarded Ambassador Rowny the Presidential Citizens Medal in 1989. The citation read: "Edward L. Rowny has been one of the principal architects of America's policy of peace through strength. As an arms negotiator and as a presidential advisor, he has served mightily, courageously, and nobly in the cause of peace and freedom." He was awarded a Bronze Star Medal and three Silver Star Medals for valor and four Legion of Merit and two Distinguished Service Medals for Meritorious Service.

In 1992, Rowny published *It Takes One to Tango,* an anecdotal account of his service to five Presidents: Nixon, Ford, Carter, Reagan, and Bush. The Polish translation of his book titled *Tango z niedzwiedziem* appeared in 2007. In 1973 he was named a Distinguished Military Graduate of West Point.

In 1992 Rowny fulfilled a 50-year ambition by heading the honorary committee which planned and carried out the return of Ignacy Jan Paderewski's remains to Poland. He continues to promote the legacy of Paderewski, largely through the Paderewski Scholarship Fund, which he established in 2004.

ANDREW V. SCHALLY (b. 1926)
Nobel Prize Winner for Medicine

Endocrine oncologist Dr. Andrew Schally is the discoverer of hypothalamic hormones. For his work he shared the Nobel Prize for Medicine in 1977. He subsequently pioneered the application of analogs of hypothalamic hormones in the field of cancer treatment. Since 1978 Dr. Schally has been working intensively on hormone-dependent tumors. Today, thousands of cancer patients worldwide are benefiting from Dr. Schally´s work.

He was born in Vilnius on November 30, 1926, being of Polish, Austro-Hungarian, French, and Swedish ancestry. His father, a professional soldier had to leave the family when World War II broke out to fight with the Allied Forces. Andrew's life was influenced by the harsh childhood which he spent in the German - occupied Eastern Europe, but he was fortunate to survive the holocaust while living among the Jewish-Polish Community in Romania. In 1945 he moved via Italy and France to England and Scotland.

Dr. Schally received his training in England and Canada. He became a naturalized citizen of the United States in 1962 and joined the staff of the Veterans Administration Hospital in New Orleans. He was also Head of the Section of Experimental Medicine and Professor of Medicine at Tulane University School of Medicine. After hurricane Katrina, Dr. Schally was transferred to the VA Medical Center at Miami, Florida. At present he is Chief of the new Endocrine, Polypeptide and Cancer Institute at the VA Medical Center in Miami, Distinguished Medical Research Scientist of the Veterans Affairs Department and Distinguished Miller Professor of Pathology and Hematology/Oncology at the University of Miami, Miller School of Medicine. Fluent in several languages, Dr. Schally has 33 awards and 22 honorary degrees to his credit and belongs to more than 40 scientific organizations worldwide. In 1978 he was listed as the most cited author in the field of endocrinology. Dr. Schally is author or co-author of more than 2,200 publications (articles, abstracts, reviews, books).

Honors: Nobel Prize in Physiology or Medicine, 1977; Elected to U.S. National Academy of Sciences, 1978; Lasker Award, 1975; Borden Award in Medical Research, 1975; Gairdner Award, 1974; Mickle Price for Practical Medical Advances, 1974; Tyler Award for Reproduction, 1975; Middleton (highest VA) Award, 1970; Endocrine Society Award, 1969; Van Meter Am. Thyroid Prize, 1969; Elected, Academy of Medicine, Mexico, 1971; Brazil, 1983; Venezuela 1986; Poland, 1994; Hungarian Academy of Sciences, 1986; Russian Academy of Science, 1991; Academy of Science, Mexico, 1998. His numerous other awards include the French *Legion d´Honneur* and various Spanish and Brazilian decorations.

MARTHA STEWART (b. 1941)
America's Most Trusted Guide to Stylish Living

From the award-winning magazine *Martha Stewart Living* to the bestselling product lines that bear her name, Martha Stewart shares the creative principles and practical ideas that have made her America's most trusted guide to stylish living. Millions of consumers rely on Martha Stewart as their arbiter of style and taste and their guide to all aspects of everyday living - from cooking and entertaining to decorating and home renovating, and much more.

Raised in Nutley, New Jersey, in a Polish-American family with six children, Martha grew up with a rich sense of her heritage. Both her father's parents and her mother's parents had immigrated to the United States from Poland. Her paternal grandparents were born in Galicia. Her maternal grandparents were born in small villages outside of Warsaw and Lublin.

Martha has always drawn inspiration from her surroundings. She developed her passion for cooking, gardening and homekeeping in her childhood home in Elm Place. Her mother, a schoolteacher and homemaker, taught her the basics of cooking, baking, canning, and sewing; her father, a pharmaceutical salesman and avid gardener, introduced her to gardening at the age of three in the family's small but orderly backyard plot.

While earning a bachelor's degree in history and architectural history at Barnard College, Martha worked as a model to pay her tuition. She was married in her sophomore year, and, upon graduating, became a stockbroker on Wall Street, where she gained her early business training. After moving to Westport, Connecticut, in 1972 with her husband and daughter Alexis, she developed a catering business that showcased her remarkable talent and originality. Her unique visual presentation of food and the elegant recipes she created for her catered events were the basis for her first book, *Entertaining,* published in 1982. Martha's business sense and creative vision is the framework for Martha Stewart Living Omnimedia, and the expansive multimedia portfolio that encompasses award-winning media and merchandise, including *Martha Stewart Living* and *Everyday Food* magazines, the nationally syndicated television show, *he Martha Stewart Show,* the *Martha Stewart Collection* of home products and more.

MSLO also publishes *Everyday Food* and *Body + Soul* magazines. *Everyday Food* has a companion PBS television show and is also a book. *Everyday Food: Great Food Fast*, which is published by Clarkson Potter, became an instant bestseller when it was released in March 2007. In addition, Martha is the author of dozens of bestselling books on cooking, decorating, gardening and other domestic arts, including the recent *Martha Stewart's Cookies* and *Martha Stewart's Homekeeping Handbook: The Essential Guide to Caring for Everything in Your Home.*

MICHAL URBANIAK
(b. 1943)
American Legend of Polish Jazz

Michal Urbaniak started his musical education during his high school days in Lodz, Poland and continued in Warsaw. In 1962 he toured the USA with the band "The Wreckers", playing at festivals and clubs in Newport, San Francisco, Chicago, Washington, and New York City. After returning to Poland, he worked with Krzysztof Komeda's quintet (1962-1964). They went to Scandinavia where Urbaniak stayed until 1969. While being there he created a band with Urszula Dudziak and Wojciech Karolak, which achieved considerable success. After his return to Poland he founded "Michal Urbaniak Group" to which he invited, among others, Adam Makowicz (piano) and Urszula Dudziak (vocals). They recorded their first international album, *Parathyphus B*, and played at many festivals. At the Montreux'71 festival, Urbaniak was awarded "Grand Prix" for the best soloist and a scholarship at Berklee College of Music in Boston. After many triumphant concerts in Europe and the USA, he immigrated to the United States with Urszula Dudziak in September 1973.

Michal Urbaniak is one of the biggest jazz stars - violinist, saxophonist, composer, arranger, and developer of young talents. His international fame came with the *Tutu* album recorded with Miles Davis. He has co-performed frequently with such famous jazz masters as Quincy Jones, Billy Cobham, Stephane Grappelli, Joe Zawinul, Herbie Hancock, Wayne Shorter, Kenny Garrett, George Benson, Marcus Miller, Jaco Pastorius, Toots Thielmans, Kenny Kirkland, Larry Coryell, Lennie White, and Alphonze Mouzon. He is a creator, leader, composer and arranger of his own projects: *Jazz Legends*, *Fusion*, *Urbanator*, *UrbSymphony*. Urbaniak has performed several times at Carnegie Hall and at many famous world and NY jazz clubs like Blue Note, Village Vanguard, Sweet Basil. He has received awards, has been a winner of numerous foreign plebiscites and in 1992 his name appeared in first place in the prestigious *Down Beat* jazz magazine in 5 categories among the biggest jazz stars. He has recorded over 60 albums.

FRANK WILCZEK (b. 1951)
Nobel Laureate for Physics

Professor Frank Wilczek is considered one of the world's most eminent theoretical physicists. He is known, among other things, for the discovery of asymptotic freedom, the development of quantum chromodynamics, the invention of axions, and the discovery and exploitation of new forms of quantum statistics (anyons). When he was only 21 years old and a graduate student at Princeton University, he (in cooperation with David Gross) defined the properties of color gluons, which hold atomic nuclei together.

Professor Wilczek, a second-generation American, was born in Mineola, NY. His father's parents immigrated from Poland, and his mother's from Italy. He was educated in a New York City public school. Professor Wilczek obtained his B.S. degree from the University of Chicago and his Ph.D. from Princeton University. He taught at Princeton from 1974 until 1981. During the period 1981-88, he was Chancellor Robert Huttenback Professor of Physics at the University of California at Santa Barbara, and the first permanent member of the National Science Foundation Institute for Theoretical Physics. In the fall of 2000, he moved from the Institute for Advanced Study, where he was the J.R. Oppenheimer Professor, to the Massachusetts Institute of Technology, where he is the Herman Feshbach Professor of Physics. Since 2002, he has been an Adjunct Professor in the Centro de Estudios Científicos of Valdivia, Chile. Wilczek was married to Betsy Devine and they have two daughters, Amity and Mira.

Professor Wilczek has been a Sloan Foundation Fellow (1975-77) and a MacArthur Foundation Fellow (1982-87). He has received UNESCO's Dirac Medal, the American Physical Society's Sakurai Prize, the Michelson Prize from Case Western University, and the Lorentz Medal of the Netherlands Academy for his contributions to the development of theoretical physics.

In 2004 he received the Nobel Prize for Physics, along with H. David Politzer and David Gross for their discovery of asymptotic freedom in the theory of the strong interaction. In 2005 he was awarded the King Faisal Prize. He is a member of the National Academy of Sciences, the Netherlands Academy of Sciences, the American Academy of Arts and Sciences, and the American Philosophical Society. He has served as a Trustee of the University of Chicago. He contributes regularly to *Physics Today* and to *Nature*, explaining topics at the frontiers of physics to wider scientific audiences. He received the Lilienfeld Prize of the American Physical Society for these activities. Two of his pieces have been anthologized in *Best American Science Writing* (2003, 2005). Together with his wife Betsy Devine, he wrote a beautiful book, *Longing for the Harmonies* (W.W. Norton). His new book, *The Lightness of Being: Mass, Ether, and the Unification of Forces* (Perseus) appeared in September 2008.

WARREN WINIARSKI (b.1928)
The Man who Put Napa Valley on World Wine Map

In August of 1964 having overcome lots of problems with the old Chevrolet car which was not strong enough to pull the trailer filled with clothes, furniture and household goods and having survived the unbearable heat in Arizona Warren Winiarski, his wife Barbara, and two small children finally made their way to the Napa Valley. A week before, they had left Chicago to start a new life on the West Coast which was to bring them honor, wealth and the opportunity to catapult California and the Napa Valley on the world wine map.

Winiarski was born in Chicago in 1928 and grew up in a large Polish section on the northwest side of the Windy City. After high school Warren entered the University of Chicago, but after a short time he went to the School of Agriculture and Mining at Fort Collins in Colorado. From there he transferred to St. John's College in Annapolis, Maryland where he graduated in 1952. Among the students in Annapolis he met an aspiring painter Barbara Dvorak who would become his wife.

After graduating Warren went back to the University of Chicago for graduate studies in political science. He spent the next year in Italy doing research in political theory. While studying in Italy, Winiarski acquired an appreciation for wine as a daily accompaniment to meals. After returning from Europe, he worked at the University of Chicago as a lecturer. While working towards his PhD his interest in wine grew, turning into an obsession with vine making. He started making his own wine in his faculty-housing apartment. Finally, in 1964 the family moved to California to fulfill the destiny of his family name - Winiarski means in Polish "winemaker's son". The new winery received international recognition just four years after its establishment at the historic *Judgment of Paris* where its 1973 Cabernet Sauvignon, which was only his second vintage, won first place among the French and California wines in blind tasting. To everyone's amazement, nine leading French wine experts could not tell the French and the American wines apart. Thinking Winiarski's wine was French they selected it as the best red. California bested France and this success fundamentally transformed how Californian wines were viewed worldwide. The winning wine made top-ten wish lists and is selling for $400 to $500 a bottle. A bottle of 1973 Stag's Leap Wine Cellars Cabernet Sauvignon is now in the Smithsonian National Museum of American History.

In 1986 Winiarski acquired Nathan Fay's vineyard and in 1996 he bought the nearby Arcadia Vineyard, with its unique shell endowed soils for outstanding Chardonnay. The fame of Winiarski's wine reached the White House where the wines of Stag's Leap Wine Cellars were served during the visits of Polish Presidents there.

Winiarski has contributed to a number of publications; he has been the keynote speaker at symposiums worldwide; each summer he leads a weeklong seminar at St. John's College in Santa Fe, New Mexico. His philanthropic interests include the Statue of Liberty-Ellis Island Foundation and the Smithsonian.

In September 2007, because - as he put it - " he gave up the idea he was going to live forever", Winiarski sold his winery to a joint venture Ste. Michelle and Marchese Antinori for a whopping sum of ….. shh … .

ALEKSANDER WOLSZCZAN
(b. 1946)
Discoverer of the First Planets beyond Solar System

Professor Alexander Wolszczan is an astrophysicist whose research interests include experimental gravitation, pulsars, physics of dense matter and planetary astronomy. He received a doctorate in physics in 1975 from Nicolaus Copernicus University in Torun, Poland. He held positions at Max-Planck-Institut für Radioastronomie in Bonn, Germany, the National Astronomy and Ionosphere Center operated by Cornell University and Princeton University. At present, he is an Evan Pugh Professor of Astronomy and Astrophysics at the Pennsylvania State University and a professor at the Centre for Astronomy at Nicolaus Copernicus University in Torun, Poland.

His most important achievements are discoveries of pulsars, including the detection and characterization of a binary pulsar that has become one of the most precise probes of relativistic gravity and, in 1992, the discovery and confirmation of three planets circling a neutron star.

The neutron star planets are the first ones ever found beyond the Solar System and the first new planets detected since Tombaugh's discovery of Pluto in 1930. Wolszczan has confirmed their existence by an experimental demonstration that the predicted gravitational perturbations between the two larger planets do exist. A confirmed discovery of the first extrasolar planetary system has provided a long awaited breakthrough for planetary search programs, followed by a series of detections of giant planets around Sun-like stars by optical astronomers. The existence of planets around a neutron star demonstrates that Earth-mass planets do exist beyond the solar system and that the planet formation mechanism must be universal enough to produce planets around different types of stellar objects. The consequences of this fundamental discovery reach far beyond the field of astrophysics.

Prof. Wolszczan has received numerous awards including the Annual Award of the Foundation for Polish Science in 1992, the Alfred Jurzykowski Foundation Award in 1993, "The Best of What's New" Grand Award of the Popular Science Magazine in 1994, the Penn State Faculty Scholar Medal for Outstanding Achievement in 1995, the Beatrice M. Tinsley Prize of the American Astronomical Society. He is the recipient of the Commander Cross of the Order of Merit awarded by the President of Poland in 1997. Alexander Wolszczan is featured on one of the series of sixteen postage stamps issued in Poland in 2001 to commemorate the Polish Millennium. He has become an honorary citizen of the Polish cities of Szczecin in 2006 and Torun in 2008.

Prof. Wolszczan is a corresponding member of the Polish Academy of Sciences, and a member of the American Astronomical Society, the International Union of Radio Science, the International Astronomical Union, the American Association for the Advancement of Science, the Polish Institute of Arts & Sciences of America, and the World Innovation Foundation.

STEVE WOZNIAK (b. 1950)
Inventor of Apple Computers

A Silicon Valley icon and philanthropist for the past three decades, Steve Wozniak helped shape the computing industry with his design of Apple's first line of products the Apple I and II and influenced the popular Macintosh. In 1976, Wozniak co-founded Apple Computer with the Apple I computer. The next year he introduced his Apple II personal computer, featuring a central processing unit, a keyboard, color graphics, and a floppy disk drive with which he contributed to the launching of PC industry.

His ancestors came from Poznan in Poland in early 1870's and settled in the village of Posen, Michigan. The original settlers of Posen were all from Poland. This village located on just 1 square mile in southeastern Presque Isle County still has a strong Polish-American representation among its 300 inhabitants. Steve's parents are the late Jerry Wozniak, a very noted engineer with Lockhead, and Margaret Kern. He has a younger sister Leslie, and brother Mark. In February 1981 Steve Wozniak crashed his Beechcraft Bonanza while taking off from Santa Cruz Sky Park. As a result of the accident, he had retrograde amnesia and temporary anterograde amnesia. He had no recollection of the accident and, for a while, did not even know he had been involved in a crash. He began to piece together clues from what people told him. When his girlfriend told him about the event, his short-term memory was restored.

For his achievements at Apple Computer, Steve was awarded the National Medal of Technology by the President of the United States in 1985, the highest honor bestowed on America's leading innovators. In 2000 Steve was inducted into the Inventors Hall of Fame and was awarded the prestigious Heinz Award for Technology, The Economy and Employment for "single-handedly designing the first personal computer and for then redirecting his lifelong passion for mathematics and electronics toward lighting the fires of excitement for education in grade school students and their teachers."

After leaving Apple in 1985, Wozniak has been involved in various business and philanthropic ventures, focusing primarily on computer capabilities in schools and stressing hands-on learning and encouraging creativity for students. Making significant investments of both his time and resources in education, Wozniak "adopted" the Los Gatos School District, providing students and teachers with hands-on teaching and donations of state-of-the-art technology equipment. Wozniak founded the Electronic Frontier Foundation, and was the founding sponsor of the Tech Museum, Silicon Valley Ballet and Children's Discovery Museum of San Jose.

Steve is a published author with the release of his autobiography, *iWoz: From Computer Geek to Cult Icon*, in September 2006 by Norton Publishing ("iWoz" is one of the nicknames of Steve Wozniak - a reference to the ubiquitous naming scheme for Apple products; his other nicknames include: "The Woz" and "Wonderful Wizard of Woz").

MORE ICONS

Grazyna Auguscik (b. 1955) - one of the most intriguing vocalists on today's world jazz scene; her professional music career began in Europe, she completed her studies in 1992 at the prestigious Berklee College of Music in Boston, and has since become a prolific collaborator sharing the stage with many jazz notables; since 1994 Grazyna has made Chicago her home where she performs at the legendary Green Mill, the Chicago Cultural Center, the Millennium Park, Chicago Jazz Festival and the World Music Festival; Grazyna has recorded fourteen albums.

Christine Baranski (b. 1952) - actress; made her mark on Broadway by starring in such plays as *The Real Thing*, *Hurlyburly*, *The House of Blue Leaves*, *Rumors, Regrets Only* and *Follies which* earned her Tony Awards and a number of other honors; best-known by television lovers for her supporting role as Cybill Shepherd's hard-drinking friend Maryanne on the long-running CBS sitcom *Cybill;* her film credits include *Jeffrey*, *The Birdcage*, *Chicago* and *Cruel Intentions, Bowfinger, Falling for Grace, Mamma Mia!,* and others.

Stanislaw Baranczak (b. 1946) - poet, translator, literary critic, scholar, professor of Harvard University; he lectured on Polish literature at Harvard from 1981 and was editor of *The Polish Review* from 1986 to 1990; he was a co-founder of *Zeszyty Literackie* (a Polish literary periodical started in Paris) in 1983; a leading poet in the "New Wave" and one of the outstanding Polish writers to begin his career in the communist period; most prominent translator in recent years of English poetry into Polish and of Polish poetry into English.

Piotr Chomczynski (b. 1942) - internationally renowned expert in biotechnology, molecular biology and pharmacology; regarded as one of the "Giants of Science", i.e. the elite researchers whose work has most influenced biomedical research in the years 1983 - 2003; his study published in 1987 has been rated the world's most cited publication in these two decades (almost 50 thousand citations); the work for which Chomczynski is recognized so much describes a method he invented for extracting cellular RNA; he is the owner and president of the Molecular Research Center, Inc. in Cincinnati, Ohio; he avidly collects Polish art - his private collection consists of over 300 paintings.

Adam Didur (1874-1946) - opera singer; on November 14, 1908, Didur debuted in the title role in *Mefistofele* at the Manhattan Opera in New York; two days later, at the opening of the season at the Metropolitan, he was Ramifies in *Aida*; for subsequent 25 years he remained a principal bass of the Metropolitan Opera where he sang 729 times.

Henry Dmochowski - Saunders (1810-1863) - successful portrait sculptor; he spent almost a decade in America; he is the author of the marble busts of the Polish heroes of American Revolutionary War Tadeusz Kosciuszko and Kazimierz Pulaski located in the Congress rotunda.

Urszula Dudziak (b. 1943) - jazz vocalist; gifted with a remarkable five-octave vocal range, Dudziak employs electronic devices to extend still further the possibilities of her voice; she worked with leading contemporary musicians and was a member of the Vocal Summit group, with Jay Clayton, Jeanne Lee, Bobby McFerrin, Norma Winstone, Sting, Michelle Hendricks, and Lauren Newton; her 1970s song *Papaya* gained widespread popularity in Asia and Latin America in 2007.

Agnieszka Holland (b.1948) - film and TV director and screenplay writer; recognized for her highly political contributions to Polish New Wave cinema; Holland's best-known and well-regarded film was *Europa Europa* (1991); her later films include *Olivier, Olivier* (1992), *The Secret Garden* (1993), *Total Eclipse* (1995), *Washington Square* (1997), the HBO production *Shot in the Heart* (2001); *Julia Walking Home* (2001); *The Healer* (2004) and, *Copying Beethoven* (2006).

Mieczyslaw Horszowski (1892-1993) - pianist, lived and worked in New York City, taught at the Curtis Institute in Philadelphia; Horszowski, who had the longest career in the history of the performing arts, continued giving concerts until shortly before his death, which occurred in Philadelphia one month before his 101st birthday.

Leonid Hurwicz (1917-2008) - economist and mathematician; graduate of Warsaw University; he began teaching at the University of Minnesota in 1951 where he became a professor of economics and mathematics; he was a visiting professor at Harvard, Northwestern University, University of California, California Institute of Technology, University of Michigan, University of Illinois; in 2007 he shared the Nobel Prize in economics with two other scientists for laying the foundations of mechanism design theory; at age 90, he was the oldest person ever to win a Nobel.

Sebastian Janikowski (b. 1978) - an American football placekicker who currently plays for the National Football League's Oakland Raiders; his nicknames are: *the Polish Powderkeg*, *the Polish Cannon*, *Sea Bass*, *Lightning Feet* and more recently *the Polish Hammer*; he is widely considered to be the most powerful kicker currently in the league and leads the NFL in kickoffs for touchbacks.

Erazm Jerzmanowski (1844-1909) - the man who „illuminated America"; he discovered an original method to power lights and lamps with the energy from coal; with his many patents he moved to New York where he contributed greatly to establishing gas works which powered gas lighting throughout the city; New York City became illuminated between 1873 and 1882; then Jerzmanowski founded one gas company after another and soon the light was shining in the streets of Chicago, Baltimore, Indianapolis, Troy, Memphis and other towns; he became incredibly rich; at the end of the 19th century his fortune was estimated to be the third largest in the United States.

Bronislaw Kaper (1902 - 1983) - a film composer who scored films and musical theater in Germany, France, and USA; he made friends with the Austrian composer Walter Jurmann and, upon being offered a seven-year contract with MGM, they both immigrated to the United States in 1935; one of their first American films was the Marx Brothers comedy *A Night at the Opera* (1935), for which they scored the song *Cosi-Cosa*; Kaper composed the music for nearly 150 Hollywood movies, and won an Oscar for the MGM musical *Lili* (1953); he is now perhaps best remembered as the composer of the jazz standards *Invitation* and *Green Dolphin Street*.

Paul Kochanski (1887-1934) - violinist, composer, arranger; he made his American debut with the New York Symphony Orchestra in 1921; from 1924 until his death he taught at the Juilliard School of Music, heading the violin faculty.

John Krol (1910-1996) - Cardinal, Archbishop of Philadelphia from 1961 till 1988; the first Polish American priest to reach the highest rank in the Roman Catholic hierarchy in the US, one of the closest advisors of Pope John Paul II.

Gene Krupa (1909-1973) - jazz drummer whose innovative style of playing fascinates musicians until today; he played with Benny Goodman Band in the 30-s, which made him a star; later he set up his own band and played with a renowned saxophonist Charlie Ventura.

Henryk de Kwiatkowski (1924-2003) - member of the Royal Air Force who became an aeronautical engineer; after coming to the United States in 1957 he established De Kwiatkowski Aircraft Ltd. and Intercontinental Aircraft Ltd. headquartered in New York City making his fortune through leasing and brokering the sale of used commercial airplanes; he owned Calumet Farm, one of the most prestigious Thoroughbred horse breeding and racing farms in the United States.

Tamara de Lempicka (1898-1980) - art deco painter, portraitist; she painted European royalty and celebrities; Madonna - a great lover and collector of Lempicka's paintings - used her works in her music videos., e.g. *Open Your Heart*, *Express Yourself*, *Vogue and Drowned World/Substitute for Love*.

Tara Lipinski (b. 1982) - figure skater, Olympic Gold Medalist; at the age of 15, she won the Olympic gold medal in figure skating at the 1998 Winter Olympics, and remains the youngest gold medalist in the history of the Olympic Winter Games.

Stefan Mierzwa (Steve Mizwa) (1892-1971) - writer, scholar; in 1925 he founded The Kosciuszko Foundation dedicated to promoting and strengthening understanding and friendship between the peoples of Poland and the United States through educational, scientific, and cultural exchanges and other related programs and activities.

James Allen Miklaszewski (b. 1949) - known as Jim or "Mik" Miklaszewski; chief Pentagon correspondent for NBC News; on September 11, 2001 he was the first at the scene to report that the Pentagon had been attacked; since joining NBC in 1985, Miklaszewski was a White House correspondent during the Bush Sr. and Clinton administrations; prior to joining NBC News, he worked for CNN as a National Correspondent and covered the Reagan White House; he was also a moderator for two CNN public affairs programs, *Election Watch* and *Newsmaker Sunday*.

Julian Ursyn Niemcewicz (1757-1841) - writer and gen. Kosciuszko's aide-de-camp during the insurrection of 1794; he left for the United States with Kosciuszko in 1797; he settled in Elizabeth, N.J., where he married a prominent widow; he travelled extensively around the country keeping journals, which constitute a very interesting account of life in America at that time, published as *Under Their Vine and Fig Tree: Travels Through America in 1797, 1799, 1805, with some further account of life in New Jersey*; in 1798 he visited George Washington in Mount Vernon and in his diaries he provided a valuable look at the home life of the retired President becoming his first biographer.

Piotr (Peter) Nowak (b. 1964) - former Polish soccer player, in 1998 he moved to the United States to play in Major League Soccer for the Chicago Fire; in their inaugural season, he led the Fire to a victory in the MLS Cup and was soon recognized as one of the best players in the league; he also led the Fire to two US Open Cup victories; in 2003 Nowak was appointed as head coach of D.C. United; he quickly led D.C. to their fourth MLS Cup; currently Nowak is the assistant to Bob Bradley, head coach of United States men's national soccer team; starting from August 2007 he is also head coach of Under-23 Men's national team, which competed at the 2008 Beijing Olympics.

Bohdan Paczynski (1940-2007) - Lyman Spitzer Jr. Professor of Astrophysics at Princeton University; he laid claim to two of astronomy's most spectacular advances of the late 20th century: gravitational microlensing and the origins of gamma ray bursts; author of "the Paczynski Code" - the computer code he devised in the 1960s for calculating the evolution of single stars; he was the first to suggest that gamma-ray bursters lie outside the Milky Way and revolutionized astronomy by using gravitational lensing as a tool to search for dark matter and new planets.

Ed Paschke (1939-2004) - painter, born and raised in Chicago, received master of fine arts degree from the School of the Art Institute of Chicago; Paschke was often referred to by his friends as "Mr. Chicago"; a representative of the Chicago Abstract Imagists in his works Paschke shared references to non-Western and surrealist art, appropriated images from popular culture and employed brilliant color throughout a busy and carefully worked surface.

Jim Pawelczyk (b. 1960) - former NASA astronaut; Associate Professor of Physiology and Kinesiology at Penn State University, Pennsylvania since 1995; Pawelczyk flew aboard Columbia space shuttle in April and May of 1998, logging 16 days and 6.4 million miles in space and circling the Earth 256 times.

Artur Rodzinski (1892-1958) - conductor, music director of the Cleveland Orchestra, the New York Philharmonic and The Chicago Symphony Orchestra; he also conducted the Los Angeles Philharmonic; based on this reputation he was engaged in 1937 to recruit and assemble the famed NBC Symphony Orchestra for Arturo Toscanini; it was Rodziński who conducted the NBC's very first public performance prior to Toscanini's debut with the orchestra.

Zbigniew Rybczynski (b. 1949) - film operator, director of animated films; his career in Poland began with short films, for example *Soup*, *New Book*, *Media*; these films won awards at festivals, from Krakow to Chicago and Melbourne; his 1980 film *Tango* brought him an Oscar; he has lived and worked in the USA since 1983, where he has made films like *Steps*, *Manhattan*, and *Kafka*, many using modern computer techniques.

Pat Sajak (b.1946) - television personality, former meteorologist and former talk show host, best known as the host of the American television game show, *Wheel of Fortune;* one of Sajak's philanthropies is an expansion of the Anne Arundel Medical Center in Annapolis, Maryland; he is also part-owner of Annapolis radio station WNAV 1430 and Westminster, Maryland radio station WTTR.

Jan Sawka (b. 1958) - one of the stars of the famed Polish Poster School; since 1977 he has resided in New York, where he joined the American cultural mainstream; Sawka's works are in over 60 museums around the world; he has had over 70 solo shows at international museums and galleries.

Jerzy Skolimowski (b.1938) - film director, scriptwriter, dramatist and actor; Skolimowski has directed more than twenty films since his 1960 debut *Oko wykol* (The Menacing Eye); he now lives in Los Angeles where he paints in a figurative, expressionist mode and acts occasionally in films.

Julian Starostecki (b.1919) - soldier during world War II, prisoner of the Soviet Gulag, member of gen. Ander's Corps who took part in Monte Casino battle; main constructor of Patriot missile's warhead who supervised the writing of the technical documentation of the Patriot and its assembly.

Zygmunt Stojowski (1870-1946) - pianist and composer; head of the piano department of the Institute of Musical Art in New York and piano teacher at the Juilliard School of Music; in New York he was acclaimed as a great composer, pianist and pedagogue and had the distinction of being the first Polish composer to have an entire concert devoted to his music performed by the New York Philharmonic.

Jan Styka (1858-1925) - painter; commissioned by Ignacy Jan Paderewski, he painted an enormous panorama originally entitled *Golgotha* (the Aramaic name for the site of Christ's crucifixion), which became known simply as *The Crucifixion;* measuring 195 by 45 feet, it is believed to be the biggest religious painting in the world; the work is displayed at a specially constructed building in Glendale near Los Angeles.

Loretta Swit (b.1937) - actress; her star-making role came within two years of moving to Hollywood when she inherited Sally Kellerman's vitriolic "Hot Lips" Houlihan character on TV's *M*A*S*H* (1972); she stayed with the show the entire eleven seasons and received two Emmy Awards; she has appeared in a few films including *S.O.B.* and *Beer;* Loretta was host of the 1992 cable-TV wildlife series *Those Incredible Animals*.

Alfred Tarski (1910-1983) - widely considered as one of the greatest logicians of the twentieth century; graduate of the University of Warsaw; immigrated to the USA in 1939, and taught and researched mathematics at the University of California, Berkeley from 1942 until his death in 1983; a prolific author best known for his work on model theory, metamathematics, and algebraic logic.

Witold Urbanowicz (1908-1996) - fighter ace of World War II, according to the official record he was the second best Polish fighter ace with 17 confirmed wartime kills and 1 probable; in June 1941 he was assigned the Air Attaché at the Embassy of Poland in the United States; after the war he fled to the USA; he lived in New York City, working for American Airlines, Eastern Airlines and Republic Aviation.

Matt Louis Urban (1919-1995) - Lieutenant Colonel; born in Buffalo, New York; son of Helen and Stanley Urbanowicz - a plumbing contractor of Polish heritage; Urban was a U. S. Army officer who served with distinction in World War II; he was belatedly awarded the Medal of Honor in 1980 for repeated acts of heroism in combat in France and Belgium in 1944; according to the *Guinness Book of World Records* he is the most decorated American serviceman.

Wanda Urbanska (b.1956) - nationally known author and expert on simplicity; she has helped to identify and define one of the top trends of our time; the quest for simplicity; co-author with Frank Levering of *Simple Living: One Couple's Search for a Better Life*; she hosted the PBS primetime special *Escape from Affluenza: Living Better on Less;* she was heard on NPR's *All Things Considered;* her series, *Simple Living with Wanda Urbanska*, is currently airing on PBS stations nationwide.

Bobby Vinton (b.1935) - pop singer; called the Polish Prince; from 1962 through 1972 Vinton had more Billboard #1 hits than any other male vocalist, including Elvis Presley and Frank Sinatra; he has altogether sold over 75 million records.

Stella Walasiewicz (Walsh) (1911-1980) - athlete; living in America, but being a Polish citizen in the 1932 Summer Olympics she represented Poland; during an unusually long career (over 20 years) she won two Olympic medals and some 40 Amateur Athletic Union championships and was credited with nearly a dozen world records in women's running and jumping events; she was inducted into the U.S. Track and Field Hall of Fame in 1975.

Warner Brothers - Harry (1881-1958), **Albert** (1883-1967), **Sam** (1887-1927) **and Jack** (1892-1978), four brothers who founded Warner Bros. - the third-oldest American movie studio in continuous operation; their parents immigrated from Poland in search of a better future; the three elder brothers began in the exhibition business in 1903, having acquired a projector with which they showed films in the mining towns of Pennsylvania and Ohio; they opened their first theatre, *the Cascade*, in New Castle, Pennsylvania in 1903; by the time of World War I they had begun producing films, and in 1918 the brothers opened the Warner Bros. Studio on Sunset Boulevard in Hollywood.

Henryk Wars (1902 -1977) - pop music composer; during the 1930s he wrote songs for musical comedies in Poland; he served in the defense of Poland in 1939; in 1941 he joined Polish 2nd Corps of General Anders; after being demobilized from the army in 1947, he immigrated to the United States; in the USA he changed his named to **Henry Vars** and after a period of struggling and poverty, he managed to resume his musical career; his songs were sung by Bing Crosby, Doris Day, Brenda Lee and Dinah Shore.

Carl Yastrzemski (b. 1939) - former American Major League Baseball player and member of the Baseball Hall of Fame; Yastrzemski, nicknamed **"Yaz",** played his entire 23-year career with the Boston Red Sox, "Yaz" is an 18-time all-star, the possessor of seven Gold Gloves, a member of the 3,000 hit club, and the first American League player in that club to also accumulate over 400 home runs.

Florian Znaniecki (1882-1958) - philosopher and sociologist; he taught and wrote in Poland and the United States; he was the 44th President of the American Sociological Association; Znaniecki gained international fame as the co-author with William I. Thomas of *The Polish Peasant in Europe and America;* he taught at the University of Illinois in Urbana-Champaign until his death.

ANNOUNCING ...

POLISH AMERICAN ENCYCLOPEDIA PROJECT

The Polish American Historical Association is pleased to announce the beginning of a major project to publish an encyclopedia of Polish-American history and culture. "Every major ethnic group has published an encyclopedia detailing its experiences and contributions to American society," explained Dr. James S. Pula, editor of the forthcoming publication. "Only Polish-Americans remain without a serious historical encyclopedia. It is time to preserve our heritage for our children and grandchildren." As planned, the *Polish American History and Culture: An Encyclopedia* will contain both large interpretive essays on important general topics such as community development, organizational life, religious life, holiday celebrations and participation in the labor movement along with individual biographical entries on important Polish Americans and entries on individual organizations, events, customs and other topics of interest. The completed encyclopedia will be published by McFarland Publishers, a respected commercial printer of historical works.

To be successful, PAHA needs your assistance and support for this important project to pass along Polish American heritage to our children and grandchildren, as well as the general public. You can support these efforts in two ways

1. We are in the process of compiling a list of potential entries biographies of Polish Americans who have made important contributions to American history and culture, or to the development of the Polish ethnic community in America, and topical entries such as major organizations, events or Polish American cultural aspects (Wigilia, oberek, etc.). You can help by sending your suggestions for potential entries to the editor at jpula@pnc.edu. Also, if you are interested in authoring entries, please let us know your field of expertise and if there are any specific entries or categories of entries you would be interested in authoring.

2. As you can imagine, a project of this scope will be very expensive to complete. To bring it to fruition, we need your support. Please consider a tax deductible donation to the "PAHA Encyclopedia Project" to help preserve our heritage. All donations are welcome, and will be acknowledged in the published encyclopedia. To make your contribution, send a copy of the following form today, along with your check or money order payable to the "PAHA Encyclopedia Project," to the Polish American Historical Association, Central Connecticut State University, New Britain, CT, 06050.

Contributor: Up to $49   Sponsor: $50 to $99
Patron: $100 to $499   Benefactor: $500 or more

Name: _____
(Be sure to print this legibly as you want it to appear in the published encyclopedia.)

Amount: _____

Address: _____

City: _____ State: _____ Zip: _____

E-Mail Address: _____